The New
Enchantment of America

MINNESOTA

By Allan Carpenter

CHILDRENS PRESS, CHICAGO

ACKNOWLEDGMENTS

For assistance in the preparation of the revised edition, the author thanks:
GINGER SISCO, Information Officer, Minnesota Department of Economic Development.

American Airlines—Anne Vitaliano, Director of Public Relations; *Capitol Historical Society*, Washington, D. C.; *Newberry Library*, Chicago, Dr. Lawrence Towner, Director; *Northwestern University Library*, Evanston, Illinois; *United Airlines*—John P. Grember, Manager of Special Promotions; Joseph P. Hopkins, Manager, News Bureau.

UNITED STATES GOVERNMENT AGENCIES: *Department of Agriculture*—Robert Hailstock, Jr., Photography Division, Office of Communication; Donald C. Schuhart, Information Division, Soil Conservation Service. *Army*—Doran Topolosky, Public Affairs Office, Chief of Engineers, Corps of Engineers. *Department of Interior*—Louis Churchville, Director of Communications; EROS Space Program—Phillis Wiepking, Community Affairs; Charles Withington, Geologist; Mrs. Ruth Herbert, Information Specialist; Bureau of Reclamation; National Park Service—Fred Bell and the individual sites; Fish and Wildlife Service—Bob Hines, Public Affairs Office. *Library of Congress*—Dr. Alan Fern, Director of the Department of Research; Sara Wallace, Director of Publications; Dr. Walter W. Ristow, Chief, Geography and Map Division; Herbert Sandborn, Exhibits Officer. *National Archives*—Dr. James B. Rhoads, Archivist of the United States; Albert Meisel, Assistant Archivist for Educational Programs; David Eggenberger, Publications Director; Bill Leary, Still Picture Reference; James Moore, Audio-Visual Archives. *United States Postal Service*—Herb Harris, Stamps Division.

For assistance in the preparation of the first edition, the author thanks:
Lillian Bechtel, Fergus Falls High School; Joseph Kise, Fergus Falls Junior College; Donald N. Nelson, Editor, Minnesota Journal of Education; Department of Business Development, State of Minnesota; Minnesota Historical Society; Minneapolis Chamber of Commerce; St. Paul Area Chamber of Commerce; Duluth Chamber of Commerce.

Illustrations on the preceding pages:
Cover photograph: Grand Portage National Monument, James R. Rowan
Page 1: Commemorative stamps of historic interest
Pages 2-3: Farm on Winona Bluffs, overlooking the Mississippi River, Minnesota Department of Economic Development
Page 3 (Map): USDI Geological Survey
Pages 4-5: Minneapolis/St. Paul area, EROS Space Photo, USDI Geological Survey, EROS Data Center

Revised Edition Copyright © 1978 by Regensteiner Publishing Enterprises, Inc.
Copyright © 1966, Childrens Press
All rights reserved. Printed in the U.S.A.
Published simultaneously in Canada.

1 2 3 4 5 6 7 8 9 10 11 12 R 85 84 83 82 81 80 79 78

Project Editor, Revised Edition:
  Joan Downing
Assistant Editor, Revised Edition:
  Mary Reidy

Library of Congress Cataloging in Publication Data

Carpenter, John Allan, 1917-
  Minnesota.

  (His The new enchantment of America)
  SUMMARY: Discusses the history, natural resources, places of interest, and famous citizens of the North Star state.
  1. Minnesota—Juvenile literature. [1. Minnesota]
  I. Title. II. Series.
  F606.3.C3   1978   977.6   78-8000
  ISBN 0-516-04123-1

Contents

Scientist and Indian authority Henry R. Schoolcraft had long dreamed of discovering the source of the mighty Mississippi River. In July of 1832, Schoolcraft realized his dream when his expedition came upon the lake he named Itasca, in northwestern Minnesota. This painting by Seth Eastman (from a sketch by Schoolcraft) shows the expedition landing on a small island in the lake shortly after their discovery.

A True Story to Set the Scene

TEARS BY FAIR ITASCA SHED

"We had been four hours upon the trail, now clambering up steeps, and now brushing through thickets, when the guide told us we were ascending the last elevation. . . . Every step we made seemed to increase the ardor with which we were carried forward. . . . I kept close to his heels, soon outwent him on the trail . . . with the expectation of momentarily reaching the goal of our journey. . . . On reaching the summit, this wish was gratified. . . . What had been long sought at last appeared suddenly . . . the cheering sight of a transparent body of water burst upon our view."

Here, in the words of the discoverer, was the climax of almost two hundred years of uncertainty, the goal of much searching over the centuries, and one of the triumphant successes in the history of exploration—one of the most dramatic of the many stories of the enchantment of Minnesota.

The author of the above quotation was Henry R. Schoolcraft, eminent scientist and one of the country's greatest authorities on Indians and their customs. In May, 1832, Schoolcraft, then Indian agent in the northwest, was sent to Minnesota to try to make peace between the Sioux and Chippewa Indians of the region. He thought that the journey might give him an opportunity to do something he had long dreamed about—something that others had sought to do and failed—discover the source of the Mississippi River.

An expedition left Sault Ste. Marie, Michigan, on June 7 and reached Cass Lake, in northern Minnesota, on July 10. Here Schoolcraft left some of his party. Ozawindib, chief of the Chippewa, said that his hunting ground embraced the source of the Mississippi. He agreed to act as guide for the sixteen members of the expedition who were to join Schoolcraft on the final lap of the journey.

When they came to a place where the river branched into two forks, Schoolcraft was surprised; until that time, it had not been known that the upper Mississippi had two primary branches at this point. The explorers went up the smaller branch, which now bears

Schoolcraft's name, as far as Schoolcraft Lake. Then they went overland up the steep slopes where, after a tough climb, they had their first view of the "transparent body of water."

When the canoes were repaired with hot pitch, they were put into the lake, "and the little flotilla of five canoes was soon in motion, passing down one of the most tranquil and pure sheets of water of which it is possible to conceive. . . . After passing some few miles . . . we landed at an island (now Schoolcraft Island), which appeared to be the only one in the lake."

There they had lunch and explored the island. "I inquired of Ozawindib the Indian name of this lake; he replied *Omushkos,* which is the Chippewa name of the Elk. . . . I called it Itasca."

Much confusion has followed concerning the origin of this name. Some authorities say that Schoolcraft used the Latin words for truth (veritas) and head (caput), taking the last letters, "itas," from truth and the first two letters from head, "ca," to form "Itasca"—or "true head."

However, in an Indian legend, Hiawatha's beautiful daughter I-teska was kidnapped by the ruler of the underworld; her tears were said to have started the Mississippi flowing. Schoolcraft himself told of this legend in his poem *On Reaching the Source of the Mississippi River in 1832:*

> Ha! truant of western waters! Thou who has
>   So long concealed thy very sources, flitting shy,
> Now here, now there—through spreading mazes vast
>   Thou art, at length, discovered to the eye. . . .
> As if, in Indian myths, a truth there could be read,
>   And these were tears, indeed, by fair Itasca shed.

Probably there is truth in both of these theories as to Schoolcraft's reason for calling the Mississippi's source Lake Itasca.

His account continues, "Having gratified our curiosity in Itasca Lake, we prepared to leave the island, but did not feel inclined to quit the scene without leaving some memorial, however frail, of our visit. The men were directed to fell a few trees at the head of the island . . . for erecting a flag staff. . . . I caused the United States

10

Sunset on Lake Itasca, source of the Mississippi River.

flag to be hoisted upon it. Ozawindib, who at once comprehended the meaning of this ceremony, with his companions fired a salute as it reached its elevation. . . . This symbol was left flying at our departure. . . . The flag . . . continued to be in sight for a time, and was finally shut out from our view by a curve of the lake.

"We found this curve drawn out in such a manner as to form, with the opposite shore, the channel of the outlet. . . . Unexpectedly, the outlet proved quite a brisk brook. . . . We soon felt our motion accelerated by a current and began to glide, with velocity, down a clear stream with a sandy and pebbly bottom. . . . Ten feet would, in most places, reach from bank to bank, and the depth would probably average over a foot."

Here at last, indeed, the adventurers had reached the infant Mississippi.

11

At this spot, the Mississippi River begins its long journey as a small stream flowing from Lake Itasca.

Lay of the Land

THE RUSHING OF GREAT RIVERS

Only in Minnesota, among all the states, do two of the great river systems of the continent have their source. Only in Minnesota do the waters flow to the seas of the north, the east, and the south. Twisting and turning across the map of the state are lines that represent the dividing of the waters. In Minnesota these waters are carried away by three of the continent's great river systems: Nelson, St. Lawrence, and Mississippi.

Northward flows the mighty Red River of the North. It begins officially where the Otter Tail and Bois de Sioux rivers come together at Breckenridge. From that point on the Red River forms the border between Minnesota and North Dakota. The Red is part of the huge Nelson River system, carrying its floods into remote and frigid Hudson Bay.

The high ridge, or divide, that sends these waters north enters Minnesota north of Browns Valley and wanders northward to Sevin, where it turns to the east. Near Hibbing it meets the divide that separates the two other major river systems; the northern divide then continues to the east and north and leaves the state at North Lake on the Canadian boundary. The divide between east and south runs south and then turns east to leave the state in the Nemadji State Forest.

Much of the history, romance, and even mystery of Minnesota is associated with its many rivers, especially that mightiest and most famous of them all—the Mississippi—which is born in Minnesota. For more than 150 years one of the greatest mysteries of the hemisphere concerned the source of the Mississippi. The story of all those who sought its origin and how it was finally found at Lake Itasca is most interesting.

Many are surprised to learn that the Mississippi flows both to the north and to the east in the early part of its journey, following closely the path of the divide between waters of the north and the south. From Lake Itasca to St. Paul, the Mississippi flows about 500 miles

(805 kilometers). St. Paul is known as the head of navigation on the Father of Waters.

Below St. Paul the river can be navigated all the way to its mouth, a distance of 1,596 miles (2569 kilometers). Prairie Island, south of Hastings, is the largest island in the entire course of the Mississippi. From Point Douglas to the southern border of Minnesota the Mississippi forms the boundary between Minnesota and Wisconsin. The other important eastern boundary river is the St. Croix.

The main tributary of the Mississippi in Minnesota is the Minnesota River. This is one of the few major rivers bearing the name of a state that flows for its whole length within the state. Its source is Big Stone Lake.

The St. Lawrence River system also begins in Minnesota, with the St. Louis River considered its official source. The St. Louis is Minnesota's principal river emptying into Lake Superior; the others are not very large. Other navigable rivers are the St. Croix, Rainy, and Red Lake River.

Altogether, Minnesota can boast the impressive total of 25,000 miles (about 40,200 kilometers) of rivers and streams.

SKY BLUE WATERS

Probably nothing about Minnesota is better known than its "10,000 lakes." However, this number is a modest claim, since there are now estimated to be more than 15,000 lakes of 10 acres (4 hectares) or more. Nothing under 10 acres (4 hectares) is listed officially as a lake. Minnesota has so many lakes it apparently ran out of names. There are 91 Long Lakes, 76 Mud Lakes, 43 Rice Lakes, and 40 Twin Lakes. One lake is called This Man, another That Man, and still another is called Otherman Lake. The water surface of Minnesota, including Lake Superior, covers 6,271 square miles (16,242 square kilometers)—an area larger than all of the state of Connecticut.

King of the lake waters touching Minnesota soil is, of course majestic Lake Superior. Included within the Minnesota boundaries are 2,212 square miles (5,729 square kilometers) of Lake Superior, its waters so fresh and clear that the bottom can be seen 20 to 30 feet (6 to 9 meters) away from the shore.

Red Lake, spreading its sparkling surface over 440 square miles (1,140 square kilometers), is the largest lake within the state. Although Lake of the Woods is much larger, not all of it is within the United States. The part of it that is inside the country's boundaries, however, ranks as the second largest lake within Minnesota. Another of Minnesota's great international lakes is Rainy Lake. Mille Lacs is the third largest lake in Minnesota.

One of the most interesting lakes of the state is Lake Pepin. It is formed by a natural dam in the Mississippi that expands the river into a picturesque lake. The waters of the Chippewa River, flowing

Minnehaha Falls, *by Henry Lewis. The Indians of the Minnesota region used the suffix* haha, *meaning "laughing water," for all waterfalls.*

from Wisconsin, bring down large quantities of sand and silt. These have settled across the Mississippi in such a way that an effective dam is formed, backing up the Father of Waters for 30 miles (48 kilometers) upstream, creating Lake Pepin.

The deepest lake that is entirely within Minnesota is Gabimichigami, 226 feet (69 meters) deep. Lake Saganaga is 240 feet (73 meters) deep, but it is shared with Canada.

MOUNTAINS OF THE PRAIRIE

Some of the oldest rocks on the North American continent (igneous rocks called *gabbro*) may still be seen in the Superior Upland area of Minnesota, especially at Duluth and along the north shore of Lake Superior. Here are the flattened remains of gigantic ancient mountains and what is left of the belching fury of volcanoes. Ancient mountains once soared in other parts of the state, but their remains are long covered over. No one knows how many times such mountains rose to great heights in what is now called Minnesota and then were worn away or sank out of sight.

When the lands sank low enough, the seas rolled in, and much of what is now Minnesota was covered by shallow oceans. Then as the land uplifted again, the seas receded. This happened at least three times during untold millions of years.

About a million years ago the first ice age came to Minnesota. The weather grew colder and snow continued to pile up in what is now Canada. These snows became ice and began to move southward. Most of Minnesota was covered four different times by these glaciers—enormously heavy and powerful moving ice masses. As they moved they changed the earth—carving out valleys or filling them in, cutting into the rock, and carrying fantastic quantities of boulders, rocks, sand, gravel, and soil with them. At their edges, they piled up all this material in great ridges called moraines. One of these moraines forms the divide that sends the waters to the north and south. Another example of moraines is found in the Seven Sisters, stately hills near Evansville.

When the last glacier melted, a number of very large lakes had been formed; most of these have either disappeared or have become much smaller. Greatest of these was prehistoric Lake Agassiz. At its fullest extent it extended more than 700 miles (1,127 kilometers) across what is now Canada and parts of Minnesota and the Dakotas. Lake Agassiz covered a larger area than all the Great Lakes together do today; it was as much as 700 feet (213 meters) deep.

Lake Agassiz spilled over to send mighty prehistoric Warren River rushing down, carving out what is now the Minnesota River Valley. In time, Lake Agassiz began to shrink. The various levels can be traced by the ancient sandy beaches the lake left on its former shores.

Only a few fragments of ancient Lake Agassiz still remain. Among them are Red Lake and Lake of the Woods, as well as Lake Winnipeg in Canada. The vast flats of the Red River Valley were the bed of this once mighty lake.

Another vanished glacial lake in Minnesota was mammoth Lake Duluth. Lake Superior is the gigantic "remnant" of that even larger ancestor lake. Prehistoric Lake Aitkin once covered a large area of northern Minnesota.

Glaciers formed most of the lakes that today are natural treasures of Minnesota. There are two kinds of glacial lakes. One of these is the type that formed when a river backed up behind a natural moraine dam. The other type formed when water filled the holes scooped deep into the soil by the glaciers. Glaciers even gouged lake beds in solid rock.

One relatively small region of Minnesota was never covered by the glaciers; because of this it is known as the Driftless Area. This roughly 3,000 square mile (7,770 square kilometer) part of the southeastern section of the state has rich soil called *loess*. Over the centuries this soil was brought in by the winds and deposited there. Here no boulders hamper the open sweep of the farmers' fields.

Minnesota is not a rich field for fossils. No dinosaur remains have been found. However, the bones of mammoths, mastodons, the prehistoric ancestor of the horse, and other ancient animals have been found.

THE LAND TODAY

The Driftless Area is one of the four main land regions of Minnesota today. Others include the Young Drift Plains, the Dissected Till Plains and the Superior Uplands. Less formally, the land might be described as including the rolling prairies in the southwest, the rich fields of the Red River Valley, the high timber country in the northeast, and the wooded bluffs of the southeast.

Combined, these regions add up to a total surface area of 84,068 square miles (217,735 square kilometers), making Minnesota the twelfth largest state in size. The low point of the state drops to 602 feet (183 meters) at the head of Lake Superior. Less than 50 miles (80 kilometers) away is the highest point—Eagle Mountain, 2,301 feet (701 meters), the crest of the Misquah Hills. The Sawteeth Mountains, not far from the shores of Lake Superior, form another notable highland.

The northernmost point in Minnesota is also the northernmost point of what is called the conterminous United States—that is, the forty-eight adjoining states. This northern point is known as the Northwest Angle or the Chimney. The geography of the Chimney is unique. The land portion of the Northwest Angle juts into the Lake of the Woods. It cannot be reached by land from the rest of the United States, since the only land approaches are in Canada.

CLIMATE

Some authorities have nominated Minnesota as one of the ten most healthful states of the United States. There is great variation in temperature. Temperatures generally diminish from east to west as well as from south to north. Precipitation also decreases from east to west, varying from over 30 inches (76.2 centimeters) to less than 25 inches (63.5 centimeters). Average snowfall is 42.3 inches (107.4 centimeters) per winter.

The average day of the last spring freeze is April 30, and the average day of the first fall freeze is October 13.

18

Footsteps on the Land

MINNESOTA MAN

There are no records of how or when a Minnesota teen-ager lost her life by drowning in a lake, nor is her name known, and yet she has become very famous. In 1932 a highway crew was excavating on U. S. 59 near Pelican Rapids when they found her skeleton. Her only possession was a small daggerlike instrument made from the antler of an animal. Anthropologists who examined the skeleton say she may have lain there undisturbed for as long as twenty thousand years. The discovery was given the name "Minnesota Man," and the skeleton is one of the earliest of its kind found in the country. It is referred to by laymen as "The Lady of the Lake."

In a gravel pit in Browns Valley another skeleton was discovered; this came to be known as "Browns Valley Man." He apparently lived about twelve thousand years ago. His features are thought to have resembled those of the Eskimo of Greenland.

More than ten thousand mounds made by prehistoric peoples of Minnesota have been discovered. The objects found when some of

The Indian burial mound in the lower left-hand corner of this picture is located in Itasca State Park.

This painting by Henry Lewis depicts a Dacotah Indian burial. The Dakotah, a branch of the Sioux family, were the earliest known inhabitants of Minnesota.

these were excavated have provided some information about these unknown peoples. Old village sites have thrown further light on the subject. Some early peoples built dams of stones; some were boulders weighing several tons, of a type that was not very common in the areas where they were used. How they managed to build with such heavy materials is just another of the many mysteries of prehistoric mankind.

Some prehistoric peoples were probably cannibalistic—at least during tribal ceremonies. Ruins of underground shelters dug by early people also have been found. Some of the most common remains of early peoples of many periods are pictographs—drawings made on caves or rocks. Parts of some pictographs in the Superior National Forest have been chipped away by chemists who wanted to analyze their content to see what has made their colors last so long.

CHILDREN OF THE GREAT SPIRIT

The earliest inhabitants known to us through historical records in what is now Minnesota were the Dacotah Indians, a branch of the great Sioux family. In Minnesota the Dacotah were more commonly known simply as the Sioux. As waves of European settlers forced the Ojibwa Indians to leave their ancestral homes and move westward, the Ojibwa began to move into the Sioux lands. The Ojibwa were a part of the great Algonquin nation, and in Minnesota are more commonly known as Chippewa.

The Sioux at first resisted the invaders, but were driven back ruthlessly because the Chippewa had brought with them the guns of the Europeans. The warfare between Sioux and invading Chippewa continued for generations, as both sought to possess the finest lands and the richest hunting.

The Chippewa were originally forest dwellers. They were shorter than the Sioux and had developed great endurance through the hard life in the forests. The Sioux were plains people. The buffalo was their principal source of food. They used the skins for tepees, robes, clothing, and many other necessities. Before early European explorers introduced horses on the plains, the plains Indians hunted on foot. Later they became most extraordinary horsemen.

Buffalo tongue was considered a delicacy, and the hump behind the shoulders was also thought to be choice. The meat not immediately needed was pulled into fine pieces, boiled, and placed in a bag of buffalo skin which lined a hole in the ground. The meat was pounded as tightly as possible into the bag in the hole. Hot buffalo fat was then poured into the sack, sealing the meat tightly to preserve it from the air. Then the sacks were closed by sewing. This dried, compressed meat was known as pemmican; experts say it was one of the most nourishing foods known, and it could be kept for long periods, sometimes for years. For the forest Indians the deer was as great a necessity as the buffalo was for the plainsmen.

Another food that was dried and stored by the Indians in Minnesota was the blueberry. Dried blueberries were used when no fresh fruit was available

The Indians used more than forty plants for food. A flour to thicken gravy was made from berries and leaves of the bearberry. Dried cornsilk sometimes substituted for salt. Pumpkin, squash, celery, bulrush roots, basswood sap, and even mosses provided food or needed materials.

Probably the most important plant was wild rice. The extensive shallow marsh bottoms were frequently covered with waving plumes of heavy wild rice grains. Indian women and children moved through these marshes in canoes, pulling the heads of the grain over the canoes and shaking the ripe grain into the craft. This practice is followed even today.

Indian men would tread barefoot on the rice to separate the grain from the chaff. This was the only work considered fit for Indian men to do. All other manual labor (except hunting and warfare) was carried on by women.

Seth Eastman's painting of the Indian rice-gatherers of Minnesota. Indians of Minnesota today gather rice in the same manner their ancestors did.

The Chippewa knew how to tap the hard maple tree for its sweet syrup and how to boil this down to make delicious maple sugar.

The dome-shaped wigwams of the Chippewa were made by covering poles with sheets of birchbark or woven mats of reeds or grass. Most Chippewa clothing was made from rabbit fur, deer skin, or other animal hides. Their moccasins had soft soles and a gathered or puckered top. The word Ojibwa means "puckered," and the tribal name is thought to be taken from their moccasin style. In winter they traveled by dogsled or on snowshoes.

Their miraculously light birchbark canoes are considered one of the most efficient devices ever made by man. In *The Song of Hiawatha,* Henry Wadsworth Longfellow gave a picturesque description of canoe building, as Hiawatha called:

> Give me of your bark, O Birch-tree!
> I a light canoe will build me.
> Give me of your bough, O Cedar!
> Give me of your roots, O Tamarack!
> Into his canoe he wrought them
> Thus the Birch Canoe was builded
> And the forest's life was in it
> All the lightness of the birch-tree,
> All the toughness of the cedar,
> All the larch's supple sinews;
> And it floated on the river
> Like a yellow leaf in Autumn
> Like a yellow water-lily.

Canoes were made in many sizes; one visitor asked the Indians to make him a canoe at least 30 feet (9.1 meters) long and 5 feet (1.5 meters) wide, which they were able to do.

Generally the Sioux were not familiar with birch canoe making. They used the more awkward buffalo-skin bull boat. Both Sioux and Chippewa carried babies in cradleboards, and the Sioux pulled loads on an arrangement of sticks, called a *travois,* which was dragged behind a horse.

The region's Indians did beautiful work in stone from the famed Pipestone quarries. The soft red stone from these quarries was used by the Indians to create magnificently carved stone peace pipes, called *calumets.* Carved pipes from the Pipestone quarries have been found in many far-off places of the continent.

According to Indian legends, the Great Spirit created mankind at the quarries. The Indians agreed that the dark red stone must have been used to make their flesh. The quarry region became a sacred area where all Indian groups were allowed to cut the stone for their calumets.

The peace pipe was smoked by the men as they sat in a solemn circle—first the chief, then all others. If the promise of peace was to be especially binding, all would smoke the pipe again, passing it from one to another. Dried dogwood leaves, called *kinnikinnick,* were smoked until tobacco (much prized) was introduced.

Many of the Indian ceremonies were concerned with giving away property. The more a man gave away, the more highly his neighbors regarded him.

Jonathan Carver described many Indian customs, including the burial of a chief. He was dressed in his richest robes and most decorative moccasins; eagle feathers in his hair indicated the number of enemy braves he had killed. He was buried in a sitting position. When the German poet Schiller read Carver's description, he was inspired to write a poem.

The Minnesota Indians were not lacking poetry of their own, such as the poignant Chippewa *Farewell to the Warriors:*

> Come,
> It is time for you to depart.
> We are going on a long journey.

Indian authority Frances Densmore wrote, "It was the custom for the women to accompany the warriors a short distance, all singing this song; later the song would be heard again, faintly at first, then coming nearer as the women returned alone, singing still, but taking up the burden of loneliness which is woman's share in war."

Probably the early Indians of the region now called Minnesota are better known than any other group because of the unusual amount

Left: A George Catlin painting of some magnificent pipes and peace pipes, carved by the Indians of the Minnesota region from the soft red stone of the Pipestone quarries.
Below: Catlin's painting of the Pipestone quarries in Minnesota.

of literature about them. *The Song of Hiawatha,* Longfellow's poem, is one of the most popular pieces of literature of all time. To most people the early Indians of Minnesota became as familiar as old friends.

The names of Minnetonka and Minnehaha have become a part of the general language. The Indians of the region used the suffix "haha" for all waterfalls, for this was "laughing water." Indian names dot today's map of Minnesota as a reminder of the people who once called the land their own.

HOAX OR EXCITING TRUTH?

In 1898 Olaf Ohman, a Minnesota farmer of Swedish descent, stumbled onto one of the most exciting and controversial discoveries ever made. Ohman dug out a slab of graywacke stone from under the roots of a poplar tree on his farm four miles (six kilometers) northeast of the village of Kensington. On the stone were markings that looked like writing. Since no one could read the markings, Ohman used the stone as a doorstop for one of his sheds. A Wisconsin scholar, Hjalmar R. Holand, heard about the stone and became interested in it.

Holand claimed the inscription was written in runes, a kind of character writing used in Scandinavia up to the thirteenth century. He made this translation of the runic words:

"Eight Goths (Swedes) and twenty-two Norwegians, on a journey of discovery from Vinland westward. We had a camp by two skarries (islands) one day's journey north of this stone. We were out fishing one day. When we returned home, we found ten men red of blood and dead. Ave Virgo Maria. Save us from evil." On the edge of the stone was this inscription. "(We) have ten men by the sea to look after our ships fourteen days' journeys from this island. (In the) year (of our Lord) 1362."

Many scholars have concluded that Norse explorers reached North America as early as A.D. 1000. However, there has been no undisputed proof of this. If the runestone found at Kensington could

26

The Kensington runestone, discovered in 1898 on a Minnesota farm, may indicate that Norse explorers reached Minnesota more than one hundred years before Columbus made his voyage to the New World.

be believed, this would be proof that hardy Scandinavian explorers had penetrated inland the unbelievable distance necessary to reach what is now central Minnesota more than a hundred years before Columbus made his voyage.

Is this a true account of a dramatic exploration of tremendous historical importance, or was it simply a clever hoax designed by an unknown person whose motives were equally unknown? The question has caused one of the great arguments of our time, and the truth may never be fully known.

Holand was an authority on Scandinavian history of the middle ages, and after long study he was convinced that the runestone was an authentic record. He spent much of his life until he died in 1963 trying to prove this point. He pointed out that the roots of the tree had wrapped themselves around the stone, and the tree was shown to be at least seventy-two years old, so that if the stone were a hoax, it must have been placed there at a rather early time in the modern history of Minnesota.

Actual Norse implements of the fourteenth century were found in Minnesota along the route the Norsemen must have traveled. Authenticated by experts, these included two axes, a spear, a fire-steel, two ceremonial halberds, and thirteen other implements proved to be over six hundred years old and of Norse medieval origin.

Along the same route have been found several holes chiseled into stones on lake shores. These were identical with those used by the

27

early Norwegians to moor heavy boats. Holand predicted that one of these should be found on Big Cormorant Lake, and later such a stone was discovered there.

The accounts refers to "this island." Although the region is now farmland, geologists think that at one time it was covered by a lake and that the place where the stone was found would have been an island at one time. The stone appears to have weathered for a long time.

However, the strongest argument for the truthfulness of the writing seems to be the fact that it is so skillfully done that it would have been impossible for anyone but a brilliant scholar of old Norwegian writings to have been able to write it. If this were a hoax, someone of almost unbelievable skill went to a tremendous amount of trouble without any known reason for doing so.

THE FRENCH EXPLORERS

French explorer Etienne Brule may have visited the foot of Lake Superior in 1622. Other explorers, including Radisson and Groseilliers, are thought to have touched what today is Minnesota. However, the first European of record in the present state was Daniel Greysolon, who took the name Sieur du Lhut, better known today simply as Duluth.

Duluth visited the present-day Minnesota region in 1679 to try to persuade the Sioux and Chippewa to stop their constant fighting with each other. He discovered three great Sioux villages and impressed the Indians with his personal bravery, and with the mighty power of the king of France. They promised to live in peace with the people of France.

In 1680 three explorers, Accault, Du Gay, and Father Louis Hennepin, started up the Mississippi River. They were taken prisoner by a party of Minnesota Sioux, who forced them to accompany them on their way north. Father Hennepin named present Lake Pepin "Lake of Tears" after the young braves wept all night there because the older Indians would not let them kill the prisoners. Just below the present site of St. Paul they left their canoes and started overland. When the Europeans became exhausted, the Indians would set fire to the grass behind them, forcing them to hurry. In this way they journeyed over a hundred miles (161 kilometers) across swamps, through streams, and along rocky paths to the Indian headquarters at the lake now known as Mille Lacs.

For many miserable weeks the captives endured the poor food and the anxiety that their captors might decide to kill them. When Father Hennepin said his prayers, the Indians angrily demanded that he stop muttering, for they thought the words were being used as magic against them. Hennepin decided to sing his prayers, and the Indians were pleased with the music.

On a trip down the Mississippi, Father Hennepin came upon a splendid waterfall, which he named in honor of his patron saint—Saint Anthony. He is known as the discoverer of the Falls of St. Anthony, the first European to have visited the location that later became the great city of Minneapolis. Although Hennepin and his companions made many plans to escape, they were not able to carry them out.

This canoe in the museum at Itasca State Park may be like the ones used by the Sioux and their prisoners, Hennepin, Accault, and Du Gay.

Duluth, however, had returned to Minnesota and heard that Indians were holding French prisoners. He hurried to find them and caught up with them below the falls.

Duluth boldly denounced the Indians in the Sioux language. He reminded them of the treaty of friendship that had been made and demanded the release of the prisoners, to which they agreed. After returning to Mille Lacs for feasts and ceremonies, the Frenchmen set out across the wilderness and finally reached Montreal. After returning to France, Father Hennepin published *A Description of Louisiana,* which became very popular and was translated into many languages.

For many years French traders, known as *voyageurs,* threaded their way through the wilderness offering blankets, knives, mirrors, and other trinkets to the Indians in return for furs, buffalo robes, and other valuable items. By river and stream, with some portaging, these intrepid merchants could make their way into almost any part of what is now Minnesota.

There were three main waterways into the Minnesota country. A French nobleman, La Verendrye, and his sons and nephew opened the canoe route from Lake Superior to Lake Winnipeg, and were the first Europeans known to have visited the Red River Valley. The Red River-Red Lake River passage became another of the main Minnesota routes. The third was the passage across Wisconsin following the Green Bay-Wisconsin River route to the Mississippi. All of these routes were designed to connect with the French headquarters in Canada.

Trading posts were established; Fort Beauharnois was built on the west shore of Lake Pepin in 1727, and the Verendryes built Fort St. Charles on the Northwest Angle in 1732. Then in 1763, after the French and Indian War, the British gained control of the entire Northwest. In 1768 the greatest of all the Minnesota fur trading posts was established at Grand Portage. This was the principal depot of the Northwest Company, a partnership of merchants dealing in furs and other commodities. Furs came to Grand Portage from as far away as Great Slave Lake, a distance of more than 1,500 miles (2,414 kilometers).

In the heart of the wilderness Grand Portage grew into a trading "metropolis," boasting flourishing trade, good shops featuring French fashions, a police force, and many saloons. The "port" could accommodate 150 canoes. As many as 70 very large fur cargo canoes were built there in a year. Although it is now only a sleepy Indian village, some experts consider Grand Portage the oldest European settlement in Minnesota.

UNCLE SAM

After the Revolutionary War the region between Lake Superior and the Mississippi River passed into the hands of the new United States. It is strange to think that the great Benjamin Franklin made an important contribution to faraway Minnesota, which he had never visited. In the treaty after the war, Franklin insisted that the northern boundary must be farther north than the 45th parallel that the British had proposed. The present vast and valuable areas of the state north of this line are part of Minnesota because of Franklin's persuasive powers.

In 1787 the American Congress set up the famed Northwest Territory, which included land from what is now Ohio through all of what is now eastern Minnesota. In 1803 the United States purchased the Louisiana Territory from France. Now land on both sides of the Mississippi was American territory, though the exact location of the northern boundary was still unknown.

To help establish American control of the upper Mississippi region, in 1805 the United States sent Lt. Zebulon Pike with a detachment of troops. He was to explore the upper Mississippi to its source, gather information on the Indians, make peace between the Sioux and Chippewa, win the friendship of the Indians for America, and locate places for future military posts.

The winter journey up the Mississippi was filled with hardships. Even the ink froze as Pike attempted to keep the daily entries in his diary. Pike thought that he had reached the headwaters of the Mississippi when he had reached only as far as Upper Red Cedar

Lake, now called Cass Lake. At Leech Lake, where there was a trading post, Pike gathered the Indians and others together and with great ceremony raised the American flag for the first time in what is now Minnesota. As a dramatic demonstration that the British were no longer in command, he ordered the British flag shot down from its pole.

At the junction of the Minnesota and Mississippi rivers, Pike made the first American treaty with the Indians ever written in Minnesota. They agreed to release two tracts of land, one at the mouth of the St. Croix and another at the Falls of St. Anthony. As historian Bruce E. Mahan pointed out, "For 60 gallons of liquor 'to clear their throats,' and presents valued at two hundred dollars, the chiefs assented to the cession of over 100,000 acres of land."

In spite of Pike's efforts, the British traders and merchants who operated in the region continued to show contempt for the American claim to ownership, even after the War of 1812 established that ownership beyond doubt. However, by 1816 John Jacob Astor's American Fur Company had become the principal trading establishment in the region.

To protect American interests, Colonel Henry Leavenworth was sent in 1819 to build a fort on the land where the Minnesota and Mississippi rivers joined. Though this had been included in the Pike treaty, payment had never been made to the Indians. The Leavenworth party of seventeen long boats filled with soldiers made an impressive sight, and the Indians were awed. The colonel's party brought along two thousand dollars' worth of guns, powder, blankets, tobacco, and other merchandise, which was given to the Indians by Indian agent Major Forsyth. For a time, the Indians were pleased with the payment.

The troops built log buildings near present-day Mendota, and suffered many hardships through the long winter. The wives of many of the soldiers had accompanied them, and in spite of the hardships they enjoyed dances and other festivities.

In 1820 Colonel Josiah Snelling succeeded Colonel Leavenworth. Snelling chose a lofty bluff overlooking the two rivers as site for the fort. A crude sawmill was set up to process logs for the fort, and

32

Fort Snelling (above) was built on a lofty bluff overlooking the place where the Minnesota and the Mississippi rivers join. Painting by Henry Lewis.

building began. The fort was not ready for all the troops until 1824. Colonel Snelling named the fort St. Anthony; in 1825 it was renamed Fort Snelling in his honor.

One of the early events of interest at the fort was the birth of the Snellings' daughter—the first child of European parents born in what is now Minnesota. Born only a few days after Mrs. Snelling arrived, the little girl lived only slightly more than a year and was buried at the fort.

The city of St. Paul started in 1838 as a small community called "Pigs Eye" (above) on the banks of the Mississippi River. Painting by Henry Lewis.

Yesterday and Today

SNORTING BOATS AND OTHER PROGRESS

According to historian Russell W. Fridley, "with the establishment of Fort Snelling a new era began for the Minnesota country. The erection and garrisoning of the post effectively extended for the first time the authority of the young American nation over the region, paved the way for white settlement, and set in motion the transformation of a vast Indian territory into an American state. As a military outpost on the remote American frontier, Fort Snelling served as the nucleus from which stemmed the settlement of Minnesota and much of the Northwest."

One of the most important developments took place in 1823. A strange sound, like the hoarse call of a mammoth bull moose, was heard along the riverbanks. People rushed to the shore; the Indians peered down from the higher shores with mingled curiosity and horror. The first steamboat, the *Virginia,* had arrived in the upper Mississippi. The settlers cheered, and the Indians crept down for a closer view. When the whistle sounded, they fled in terror; even the strongest braves felt that this magic monster was too much for them.

Steamboats would now be able to provide the large quantity of supplies and the means of transportation needed to open up the country.

Among the earliest government representatives to have headquarters at Fort Snelling was Indian agent Major Lawrence Taliaferro. For twenty years this wise and just man was especially successful in keeping the best possible relations among Indians and Europeans. The rivalry between Sioux and Chippewa broke out in 1835, 1842, and 1845. The last battle between the two groups in Minnesota took place in 1858.

In 1820 Lewis Cass, governor of Michigan Territory, of which Minnesota was then a part, visited Minnesota and attempted to find the source of the Mississippi. Other prominent visitors included Major Stephen H. Long, who explored the Red River Valley and northern Minnesota; artist George Catlin, whose journey in 1836 took him to the famous Pipestone quarry; and Joseph N. Nicollet, whose tours in the late thirties resulted in the first accurate map of the present state. With Nicollet on his second trip in 1838 was John C. Fremont, later to become one of the best-known American explorers. An Italian traveler, Giacomo Beltrami, arrived on the first steamboat in 1823. He was not particularly successful as an explorer, but his later writings of what he had seen did much to make the Minnesota region known to the outside world.

Perhaps the best-known of all the visitors of this period was Henry R. Schoolcraft. He felt sure that the lake he had found was the long-sought source of the Mississippi, and later scientists confirmed this.

Fur trader William Morrison claimed to have discovered the great river's source in 1804, but he waited until 1856 to make his claim, and by this time it was difficult to prove his point. However, a letter he had written to his brother gives many details of the site and even describes the five small streams that empty into Lake Itasca. His claim seems to have strong foundation. However, there is no doubt that Schoolcraft was the first scientific explorer of the Mississippi headwaters.

Another important work of this period was the labor of the missionaries among the Indians. Catholic missionaries Dumoulin and Edge came to Rainy Lake and Pembina as early as 1818. Presbyterian missionaries Coe and Stevens arrived in 1829; they were followed by Congregationalists and Methodists. At present-day Minneapolis in 1834 the Pond brothers, Gavin and Samuel, set up the first mission to the Sioux.

A great achievement of the missionaries was their creation of alphabets for the Indian languages. These alphabets made it possible to convert the spoken languages to written languages. The Ponds were leaders in this work with the Sioux language.

NOT IN A PIG'S EYE

In 1838 Pierre Parrant, an unsavory character who sold whiskey and who was nicknamed "Pig's Eye," built a cabin on the present location of St. Paul. Before long, others had gathered in the vicinity, and the little community began to be called by the unfortunate name of Pig's Eye.

Fortunately, in 1841 Father Lucian Galtier built a log cabin chapel there, which he dedicated in 1841 to Saint Paul. Later he persuaded the settlers to adopt that more dignified name for their community. A later Catholic official wrote of Father Galtier, "If any one man can be said to have been the founder of this city in the beginnings of which there were many more or less concerned, the honor of the title is to be awarded to him."

In 1842 the first store in the village opened. An observer in 1843 wrote, "It had but three or four log houses, with a population not to exceed twelve white people, and was a mixture of forests, hills, running brooks, ravines, bog mires, lakes, whiskey, mosquitos, snakes, and Indians."

In 1838 Franklin Steele built a cabin on the east side of the Falls of St. Anthony and hired a man to live there. In 1844 Pierre Bottineau took out a claim next to Steele's. At this time the two men owned much of what was later to become Minneapolis. Other settlers followed, and St. Anthony, later the east side of Minneapolis, had begun to grow.

The Webster-Ashburton Treaty of 1842 established the northern boundary of Minnesota as it is today, generally.

When a land office was opened at St. Croix Falls the first large group of settlers came in. In 1849 the Territory of Minnesota was organized by Congress through the efforts of Senator Stephen A. Douglas of Illinois and Henry H. Sibley, who was Minnesota's most prominent citizen of the time. Alexander Ramsey was the first territorial governor. St. Paul was selected as territorial capital. In the same year that the territory was organized the Minnesota Historical Society was founded and today is the oldest institution in the state.

More than a month went by after the territorial bill passed in Washington before the news came to Minnesota. The ice was still in the river, and there was no way for the news to reach St. Paul. When the first steamer of the spring reached the city, the news it brought was joyfully received.

BECOMING A STATE

Until 1851 most of Minnesota remained in Indian hands. In that year the Treaty of Traverse des Sioux and later treaties of 1854 and 1855 opened much of the state for settlement, which became very rapid in the 1850s.

When the Rock Island Railroad reached the Mississippi in 1854, it decided to celebrate by inviting a large crowd of distinguished people to travel over the railroad and up the river in five large steamboats. The impressive passenger list had such familiar names as former President Millard Fillmore and historian George Bancroft. On the evening the boats passed through Lake Pepin, they were lashed together so that guests could visit from one craft to another.

Excitement in St. Paul was at its greatest height, and the visitors were much impressed by a banquet, visits to Minnehaha Falls, the Falls of St. Anthony, and Fort Snelling. The visit gave St. Paul a great boost in its race to become the "Gateway to the Northwest."

By 1857 settlement had progressed so far that statehood was a possibility. Because Republicans and Democrats could not agree on a proposed constitution, each group approved separate and different constitutions. Because many southern members of Congress would not approve a new nonslave state, Minnesota had to wait almost a year before the statehood bill was approved. On May 11, 1858, Minnesota took its place as the thirty-second state. Henry H. Sibley was elected the first governor.

During its colorful history up to this time, Minnesota had been a part of the empires of France, Spain, and England, a part of the Northwest Territory and of the territories of Louisiana, Indiana, Illinois, Michigan, Missouri, Iowa, and Wisconsin, as well as the Minnesota Territory.

THE PEOPLE AND HOW THEY LIVED

By 1860 eastern and southern Minnesota were well-settled areas. To the west, Hutchinson, Glencoe, and Litchfield were growing

Sod houses like this one at Ft. Belmont, Jackson, were built by prairie settlers who had no other materials but the sod under their feet.

rapidly. On the Minnesota River, New Ulm was a thriving little city guarded against danger by Fort Ridgely, which had been established in 1853. Above the Falls of St. Anthony on the Mississippi, settlement had reached beyond St. Cloud to Little Falls and up the valley of the Sauk River. Sauk Centre and Alexandria were stockaded settlements in the wilderness. There were a few settlers in the Red River Valley, and an isolated settlement had been formed at Duluth on Lake Superior. Much of the region was still a place of pioneering.

Where the prairie sod grew tough and strong, sometimes four oxen had to pull the plow when the soil was first broken up. The pioneers had to spend almost every moment in growing, and otherwise obtaining, enough to eat.

Where there was timber, log cabins were built for shelter. Some of the wealthier pioneers were able to bring in lumber. On the prairie the only available building material was the earth itself, so thick pieces of sod a foot or more in length were cut and used as "bricks" for walls. A few poles supported the sod roof. Many of the sod houses were partly sunk into the soil.

Many pioneers brought with them a few pieces of furniture, but much of it had to be improvised from boxes and other materials. Candles were usually homemade, and most pioneer women spun their own thread and wove their own cloth. Most of the food came from the farm and garden. The few supplies that were bought had to be shipped long distances, generally by boat up the Mississippi and then overland by wagon.

But even in the busiest times there was enjoyment. Pioneers helped one another in such big jobs as "house raisings"; the completion of the job was usually celebrated with a hoedown or other festivities. After the corn was harvested, there were cornhusking bees, and the lucky man who found a red ear was entitled to kiss the girl of his choice, if she hadn't already slipped out of the room in great embarrassment.

In communities that were lucky enough to have a country general store, a shopper could find nearly everything available at the time, and the stores provided a center where almost everyone met to discuss the topics of the day.

TWO WARS

The Republican Party grew swiftly in Minnesota, and Alexander Ramsey became governor in 1859. Many in the state were strong foes of slavery. Participating in its first national election in 1860, Minnesota voted for Abraham Lincoln with a plurality of ten thousand votes.

The newborn state was the first to respond with an offer of troops when President Lincoln called for them at the start of the Civil War. During the first Battle of Bull Run the First Minnesota Regiment had more losses than any other northern regiment and was highly praised by the War Department. The Second Minnesota Regiment played an important part in the Battle of Missionary Ridge during the action around Chattanooga, Tennessee.

40

Many war historians agree that the First Minnesota Regiment had a critical role in the Battle of Gettysburg. A reckless, suicidal charge of the regiment saved Cemetery Ridge from capture by the enemy and had a great deal to do with the Union's final success in the battle. Only about 50 men of the 262 who made the charge escaped injury or death.

In spite of its small population, Minnesota contributed more than twenty-two thousand men to the Civil War. Pioneer Minnesota was dangerously weakened by this loss of manpower.

While the war was raging far away, another bloody war came to those Minnesotans who had remained at home. The Sioux Indians had been growing more and more restless. Their corn crop failed; they accused the government agents of cheating them, and traders of taking advantage of them. Then in 1862 government payments of food were delayed by the Civil War. On August 17, four Indians became involved in an argument concerning their personal bravery. To demonstrate their courage, they killed five settlers—three men and two women.

When they hurried back to the reservation and told what they had done, many tribal leaders felt this was a good opportunity to go on the warpath. They argued all night—pointing out that most of the settlers' young men were away fighting the Civil War. The Indians felt that if they ever were to get back the lands they had lost, now was the time. At last they decided to drive out the Europeans forever, and more than fifteen hundred warriors took to the warpath under Chief Little Crow.

Bands of Sioux swept across the country, sometimes wiping out entire families, at other times taking women and children captive. For days they continued the slaughter. A region 200 miles (322 kilometers) long and 50 miles (80 kilometers) wide was wiped out.

Many sought refuge at Fort Ridgely. Little Crow attacked this outpost on August 20. Although called a "fort," the community did not even have a stockade. The terribly outnumbered defenders fought bravely; the Indians reached the outlying buildings but were driven back and finally stopped the attack when night came. They had planned to set fire to the buildings with their fire arrows, but fortunately

The Defenders' Monument in New Ulm was built in honor of the courageous Minnesotans who defended the community at Fort Ridgely against the Sioux.

it rained heavily all the night and the next day. On August 22, about 1,000 Indians again attacked the 180 defenders. The cannon of the fort helped greatly in its defense, and finally a last desperate attack was beaten back; the defenders were just about out of ammunition when the Indians retreated.

Three defenders had been killed, and Indian dead were estimated at one hundred. During the worst of the battle a baby had been born at the fort. Later the government had a special medal struck for the heroic defenders on which was inscribed *Tee-yo-pa nah-tah-ka-pee,* meaning "They kept the door shut."

Many refugees fled to New Ulm; earthworks and other fortifications were set up there. Charles E. Flandrau, former Indian agent, hurried to the town with inexperienced volunteers. The Indians attacked, screaming, whooping, and singing war songs. They did not attack in a straight line, but dashed back and forth, getting gradually closer as they protected themselves by leaning to the side of the

42

ponies. Colonel Flandrau led a sortie, or attack, of about a hundred men against five hundred Indians and routed the first day's attack. During the night the defenders made imitation cannon from stove pipe, since they knew that the Indians had a terror of cannon. The second attack was repulsed, and the "cannon" are given much credit. The striking of heavy anvils gave forth a realistic booming noise. Only twenty-five houses were left in New Ulm to shelter twelve hundred persons.

H.H. Sibley was placed in general command of the Minnesota forces against the Indians. He had been a great friend of the Indians and had even saved large numbers of them from starving; he had warned as early as 1850 that unless the Indians were better treated they probably would make trouble. He was thoroughly familiar with the Indian ways.

Sibley's troops were untrained and because of the war they had poor rifles with ammunition that did not even fit. He quickly trained the ragged troops, however, and worked on the ammunition to make it suitable. Finally, he defeated the Indians under Little Crow at Wood Lake. Three days later 269 white captives were released.

Almost 2,000 Indians were taken prisoner, and the call for revenge went up from the settlers. More than four hundred were put on trial, and more than three hundred of these were condemned to death. These were brought to Camp Lincoln at Mankato. President Lincoln carefully studied the records of the condemned prisoners. Bishop Henry B. Whipple urged the president to show mercy. The bishop had long ago pointed out that unscrupulous traders and dishonest government agents were driving the Indians to revolt; and that the government was much to blame for the Indian complaints.

Lincoln commuted the sentences of all but thirty-nine of the condemned men. December 26, when they were to be executed, found throngs of people in Mankato, with crowds at every place where the execution could be viewed. Two thousand Minnesota troops patroled the scene to keep order. At the last moment one of the thirty-nine was reprieved, and the remaining thirty-eight walked to the scaffold platform in single file, singing a war song. Each one calmly placed the noose around his own neck, and all continued to sing as the cap was put over their eyes. W.H. Dooley, whose entire family had been massacred by the Indians, cut the rope holding the trap door, and the thirty-eight prisoners dropped to their deaths. This was the largest official wholesale execution ever conducted in the United States.

The dangers of Indian attack in Minnesota were over, but six hundred settlers had lost their lives in this unnecessary bloodshed. Several of the Indians had remained friendly. Taopi, a Christian chief, risked his life to aid his European neighbors during the uprising; this act is commemorated in the book *Taopi and His Friends.* John Other Day, another Christian Indian, gathered sixty-two European refugees in an old building and led them to safety. He was given twenty-five hundred dollars by Congress for his heroic act. Congress took away most of the privileges of the Minnesota Sioux and all but about twenty-five—those who were known to be friendly—were removed from the state.

A GROWING STATE

As the state grew and developed, there was much rivalry among towns and cities. There was especially intense rivalry between Minneapolis and St. Paul. Census takers were kidnapped so that the census figures would not show one city ahead of the other in population, and rival newspapers kept the contest going. The rivalry prevented cooperation and left many worthwhile things undone.

Much of the rivalry among smaller towns was for county seats. Albert Lea was helped to gain the county seat by its favorite racehorse, Old Tom. The Itasca people lost so much money when Old Tom beat their favorite that they could not contest the county seat which was given to Albert Lea. Many county seats were won by the side that was able to get and hold the county safe or strongbox and the county records.

Much of the story of growing and modern Minnesota is related to the development of transportation, industry, agriculture, and other important affairs that are taken up in other sections of this book.

44

A terrible scourge of grasshoppers in Minnesota began in 1873. In 1876 the Lake of the Woods boundary line was at last determined. The state was plagued by land frauds. People who had some Indian blood had been given the right to certain lands. Over the years many were cheated out of these rights, and others gained control of large tracts through fraudulent use of such rights.

One of the important long-term projects in Minnesota beginning in the 1880s was the building of dams and the implementation of other means to control floods and keep the water at a high enough level during the summer months. The Upper Mississippi Reservoir System was the result of this effort.

The worst ship disaster of the region occurred in 1890 when in a storm the steamer *Seawing* capsized in Lake Pepin. Ninety-eight people were killed. In another disaster a raging forest fire that centered around Hinckley took more than 400 lives. Hero Jim Root, engineer on the Northern Pacific, saved 350 people on his train by backing it through a curtain of flame and then across the burning Grindstone Creek bridge, at last reaching safety in Duluth. The heat was so intense and the throttle had become so hot that Root's hands were fused to the throttle when the heroic task was finished.

In 1905 Minnesota proudly dedicated its outstanding new capitol building. The mammoth Superior National Forest was established in 1909 under the direction of President Theodore Roosevelt. When the Panama Canal was opened in 1915, it took away much of the trade from the Orient that had previously gone through Minnesota.

During World War I 123,325 Minnesotans were in uniform.

A tornado at Fergus Falls in 1919 killed sixty persons. During the 1920s the rise of the Farmer-Labor party was dramatic. In the election of 1936 that party gained all but two of the state offices, both of the United States Senate seats, and a majority of the Minnesota delegation in the House of Representatives.

Both the Great Depression and the drought of the 1930s brought great suffering to the people of the state. During the drought, clouds of rich Minnesota soil swirled through the air to darken the sky. Ponds, rivers, and even lakes went dry, and many communities had no water supply. However, the northwestern part of the state escaped much of the drought, and farmers from the Dakotas began to drive their herds into this region. Governor Olson sent the national guard to keep them out. Although few incidents occurred, this uneventful episode was publicized as the "Cow War." Later the rains came again and many projects were started to prevent future drought disasters.

During World War II more than 300,000 men and women from Minnesota were in the armed services, and more than 6,000 lost their lives.

In 1946 came two echoes of the historic past. On October 14 storied Fort Snelling was discontinued as a government military reservation. On November 18, the Minneapolis *Star-Journal* reported that "the Minnesota Chippewa Indians 'have laid aside their pipe of peace and decided to seek United Nations aid in the restoration of their sovereign rights to hunt, fish and trap as of old' . . . The Chippewa have indicated they will base their appeal for recognition as a sovereign minor nation on the basis that they have received recognition in the past by treaties . . . and also on the grounds of inherent rights held before the coming of the white man. . . ." The Chippewa felt this action was justified because of treatment of their claims by the United States. However, no action was taken on the appeal and the federal government set up machinery to handle claims of injustice to the Indians.

The opening of the St. Lawrence Seaway in 1959 had a tremendous impact on Minnesota. It opened the state's great ports to the ocean travel of the world, in effect bringing the ocean 1,500 miles inland. In 1961 historic Fort Snelling was dedicated as a state park, preserving the priceless old buildings in a 320 acre (130 hectare) site.

Sports fans of the state were overjoyed in 1965 when the Minnesota Twins captured the American League pennant for the first time since the team had been in the state. The fans' joy was only slightly dimmed when the Twins lost to the California Dodgers after a close World Series.

The 1970s saw a huge rise in interest and investment in taconite. The state won its great dispute with the Reserve Mining Company over the company's pollution of lake waters.

Perhaps two of the most important national events were the 1977 swearing-in of Walter F. Mondale as the forty-second vice president of the United States and the death of Minnesota's beloved senator and former vice president, Hubert Humphrey, in 1978.

News of Humphrey's terminal cancer illness brought forth an unprecedented outpouring of public honor and affection. The nation honored this selfless man before his death, rather than afterward, when he would not be able to appreciate it. During Senator Humphrey's last weeks, President Jimmy Carter flew to Humphrey's Minnesota home and escorted the senator to Washington in the presidential plane, *Air Force One.* In Washington, members of the Congress of the United States spent an entire day honoring Hubert Horatio Humphrey.

THE PEOPLE OF MINNESOTA

Minnesota is known throughout the world as a "second Scandinavia." Swedish groups were the earliest of the Scandinavian peoples. Minnesota reminded them of their home country, and they enjoyed it thoroughly. Norwegian, Danish, and Finnish settlers also came in large numbers, bringing the fine education, thrift, industry, and other qualities so characteristic of their homelands in Europe.

A large percentage of the prominent names in business, politics and government, education, and other affairs in Minnesota provides reminders of the Scandinavian past of much of the population. It is said that Minneapolis has a larger population of Scandinavian descent than any other city in the world outside of Stockholm.

Norwegians and Finns were favored in the lumber industries. When the Norwegians had earned a stake, many bought land in the Red River Valley. One of the Finnish customs from the Old World caused superstitious Americans to accuse them of worshipping pagan gods. The accusers said the Finns went from their houses dressed in sheets to worship in small wooden temples. This, of course, turned out to be the Finnish sauna bath, which has now become popular throughout the country.

The people of Minnesota today often use canoes, as did the early Indians of the region.

The Danish people first went to the southeastern section of Minnesota. They were responsible for much of the state's leadership in making butter and other milk products. Askov is the best-known Danish settlement.

The Germans and Irish in Minnesota have probably made their greatest contributions in St. Paul. New Ulm was also a center of German settlement and culture. Almost every other ethnic background is represented to some degree in the state.

Among the customs introduced have been skiing by the Scandinavians; curling by the Scottish people of Winnebago, who used their wives' flatirons for curling stones; and fox hunting by the English farmers around Fairmont.

What of those original settlers—the Indians? Today there are eleven Indian reservations and about ten thousand people of Indian blood in Minnesota, most of them Chippewa.

Some Chippewa still follow their traditional way of life—hunting, fishing, trapping mink and beaver, and harvesting wild rice. Sometimes whole families harvest rice together.

Indian children living on Minnesota reservations have the same educational opportunities as other students in the state. For this reason and others, most of the distinctions between Indians and other Minnesotans have almost disappeared.

48

Natural Treasures

One of the world's richest treasures for many years made Minnesota possibly the most important single source of raw materials in all the world. This was the vast amount of red earth that the Indians had known about even before the Europeans came. We know it today as iron ore, the basic ingredient of steel and the substance on which our whole civilization has been built for the last half century.

In the Cuyuna Range, Minnesota possesses the nation's greatest source of manganese. Minnesota also has the greatest deposits of peat of all the states. Peat deposits are found mainly in the muskegs of the north. Nowhere else in the world is the famed ruddy pipestone found. Thompsonite, jewel stones, building stone, clay, shale, mica, and feldspar are other important minerals found in Minnesota.

The vast canyon of the Hull-Russ-Mahoning open pit iron ore mine is the largest man-made hole in the world.

In addition to iron ore, the second most magnificent natural resource of Minnesota was its forest. The boundary between the eastern forestlands and the open prairies runs a little to the west of the center of Minnesota. This meant that something more than half of the present state was covered with softwood and hardwood forests when the first Europeans visited it. Total Minnesota forestland today covers about twenty million acres (more than eight million hectares). The state tree is the red pine *(Pinus resinosa),* commonly called Norway pine. This has the remarkable property of being free from both disease and insects, and lives up to three hundred years.

Most of the flowers and plants normally seen on the prairies, in the northern evergreen forests, and the more southerly deciduous forests are found in Minnesota. One of the rarest, most beautiful, and most exotic of Minnesota flowers is the state flower— *Cypripedium reginae,* the shoe of Venus the queen. Its common names are pink and white lady's slipper, or moccasin, and showy lady's slipper, or moccasin. Strangely, it cannot grow without the presence of a tiny fungus that helps the flower's roots take food from the soil. The plant grows so slowly, as do most of the orchid family to which it belongs, that ten to twenty years may pass before it can bear blossoms. It may live to be fifty years old. Once the state flower could often be seen within the boundaries of Minneapolis, but now it has become rare. Because of its many unusual qualities, the lady's slipper is one of the most unique of all state flowers.

The Indian legend of the moccasin flower tells of the lovely young Indian girl who wandered off and became trapped by a forest fire. Her mother never stopped searching for her lost daughter and finally found two beautiful blooms growing together. The blossoms were shaped just as her daugher's moccasins had been and were of the same pattern. The mother was sure she had found the burial place of her daughter, and, ever since, the Indian girl's moccasins have been growing to delight those who visit her native woodlands.

Other rare flowers in Minnesota are the fringed gentian and the fragile, almost ghostly, Indian pipes. Now scarce is the *psoralea* or Indian breadroot, which bears a tall blue spike of bloom. It once was plentiful and the roots were used as food.

Probably the most admired of all the wild products of Minnesota is *Mah-no-men,* as the Indians called the wild rice, which still grows profusely in many a watery meadowland.

Gone are the vast herds of buffalo that used to summer in the prairie lands of Minnesota and that often meant the difference between life and death for the Sioux. More numerous than ever, however, are the deer upon which the Chippewa depended. Today a vast army of hunters searches for deer in season in Minnesota. The early Indians would not have been able to believe it. In fact, it is difficult for anyone outside the state to realize that 500,000 hunters stalk the woods and prairies of the state during hunting season, not only for deer but for other game. Countless thousands watch for the spine-tingling flight of the mallard duck, listen for the haunting call of the loon, and thrill to the drumming of the ruffed grouse.

Minnesota, in fact, licenses more hunters and fishermen than any other state. Three million acres (more than a million hectares) of Minnesota fishing waters lure a million and a half fishermen every year, and sport fishermen each year spend many millions in the state trying to cure the uncurable fishing fever.

In addition to the buffalo, other Minnesota natural resources have vanished forever. Once untold millions of beautiful passenger pigeons darkened the sky as they flew by. It sometimes took hours for a single flight to pass overhead. Now they are extinct.

In order to protect and preserve the natural resources, Minnesota established a conservation board that deals with protection of all natural assets—fish, game, soil, water resources, forests, and others. Protecting forests from fires is a typical conservation task. Fires have destroyed a greater acreage of Minnesota timber than has been cut down by all the lumbermen in the many years of lumbering.

Minnesota licenses more hunters and fishermen than any other state. Many of these people travel the waters of the state by canoe.

*This ship is docked in Duluth Port on Lake Superior. The United States
government created the port in 1893. In 1976 it was the fourth
largest port in the United States, even though it is a thousand miles
from either seacoast and has a navigating season of only eight months.*

People Use Their Treasures

HIDDEN GIANTS

How was it possible for the world's largest iron ore mining complex to develop in what was at first the Minnesota wilderness? There are other regions where great quantities of high grade iron ore are known, and yet they still lie almost unused.

The answer is found in the fact that the Minnesota ore could be mined and carried inexpensively to where it could be converted into iron and steel. It was Minnesota's great good fortune that her iron mines were close enough to the vital Great Lakes waterway so that the ores could be loaded onto huge boats and carried cheaply to Indiana, Pennsylvania, and Ohio. The inexpensive coal available to those states could fire the furnaces in places where it was most economical to make iron and steel.

Reports of gold in the neighborhood of Vermillion brought a gold rush to the region, but the gold seekers found only disappointment. Then it was reported that rich iron ore had also been found near Vermillion. No iron ore rush followed; it was known that iron ore could be developed only by those who had money to build railroads to carry out the ore, and the expensive machinery required to mine it.

One such capitalist, Charlemagne Tower of Philadelphia, formed the Minnesota Iron Company in 1882. The company laid out the town of Tower and began building the Duluth and Iron Range Railroad Company. The railroad stretched from Tower, on Lake Vermillion, to Two Harbors, on the north shore of Lake Superior at Agate Bay. Miners were brought into the area, before the railroad was ready, and heavy mining machinery had to be taken apart and carried to the mines on the backs of pack animals. By mid-1884 the first shipment of iron ore from Minnesota had been made. Before long, operations on the Vermillion range extended from Ely to Tower.

During the years after the Civil War, Lewis Merritt and his seven sons became thoroughly familiar with the Mesabi hills. When their compasses behaved strangely, they were sure it was because there was iron ore in the hills that deflected the compass needles. They kept up their search for more than twenty years, and finally in 1890 Leonidas Merritt found rich iron ore. In the Indian language Mesabi means "hidden giant." The hidden giant had truly been found.

The Merritts did not have all the money needed to develop their discovery, but they tried to keep the property to themselves. By 1892 the Mesabi Range was connected by railroad to Duluth, and the first ore shipment from Mesabi went through in that year. This happened in spite of skeptics who said the Mesabi ore was so loose it could never be mined. They had in mind the old methods of digging tunnels in the earth and supporting the roofs and walls of these tunnels with timbers.

However, Leonidas Merritt worked out a much simpler system of mining the Mesabi ore; his system was known as the "open pit" method. The Merritts merely stripped the sand, clay, and boulders from the surface to get to the ore. Steam shovels scooped up the uncovered ore and dumped it into waiting railroad gondola cars.

The depression of 1893 hurt the Merritts very much, and in that year they lost control of their operation to John D. Rockefeller, who had bought a large share of their company bonds.

The mining towns of the iron ranges became rip roaring centers, as wild, probably, as any ever in the West. Hibbing soon was known as the "Iron Ore Capital of the World." When the town got in the way of the mining operations it was moved, as some have said, "overnight."

The last of Minnesota's great iron ranges was discovered by Cuyler Adams. This is the Cuyuna Range, which began production in 1911. Its unusual name comes from a man and his dog. Mr. Adams' dog was named Una; he took the first three letters of his own name, combined them with his dog's name, and came up with Cuyuna.

By 1911 Minnesota had become the national center of iron mining. The ores of Minnesota had put the United States well on the road to becoming the greatest industrial country on earth, a position based on the world's largest production of low cost iron and steel. The mining cities of Minnesota developed fine schools, parks,

54

streets, and other outstanding assets—all paid for through their extraordinary incomes from ore taxes.

Minnesota has supplied more than 50 percent of the iron ore mined in the United States. The first Mesabi ores contained as much as 60 percent pure iron ore—the richest in world history. As time has gone by the percentage of iron in a ton of ore has continued to drop. Less pure-grade ore has to be worked to maintain production. The end of iron ore mining of the old style is in sight in Minnesota.

However, there are more than 24 billion tons (21 billion metric tons) of low-grade ores, known as taconite, in Minnesota. These low-grade ores can be worked, but until recently it was so costly to do so that it was cheaper for steel manufacturers to import ore from other sources than to use taconite. Much research has gone on in Minnesota to find ways of getting the iron from taconite cheaply enough to compete with ore from other sources.

E.W. Davis, director of the University of Minnesota Mines Experiment Station, was able to develop a practical concentration process to use taconite. The world's largest taconite operation is now a reality at Babbitt and Silver Bay.

The process of making taconite usable is called "beneficiating." The ore is crushed and ground and passed beneath banks of magnets to which the small amounts of iron cling. These iron particles are pressed into pellets about the size of ping-pong balls and baked so that they hold their shape. In this form the iron is about 60 percent metal, although the original taconite might have been less than 25 percent metal.

Some experiments have been carried on using peat as fuel for smelting iron and steel. If this proves practical, the almost unlimited supplies of peat might be used to transform Minnesota into one of the world's great steel-producing centers.

FAIR TO MIDDLING

Flour milling began modestly enough in Minnesota. First commercial miller in the state was Lemuel Boles, who set up a crude mill in 1845 and, according to tradition, was forced to use part of his wife's dress for some of the sifting process.

Most of Minnesota's wheat is spring wheat. When this was ground it was so hard that a good deal of the husk, as well as the germ, remained in the flour; such flour was dark in color and likely to spoil quickly. Then a Frenchman, Edmond N. La Croix, began work in the Archibald mill at Dundas. He brought with him from Europe the secret of a new method of milling hard wheat so that those undesired "middlings" were eliminated. By 1870 this complex "middlings purifier" method of many rollers, vibrators, silk sieves, and other processes was introduced in Minneapolis. Once the plentiful spring wheat of the Red River Valley could be used, the city was on its way to becoming the "Flour City of the World." The city's rapid growth in milling was due also to the Falls of St. Anthony which provided power for the mills.

Because less wheat is grown in Minnesota, Minneapolis today ranks third in total grain milling, but it remains the headquarters for the world's five largest milling companies, including Pillsbury and General Mills. In 1960 General Mills introduced a new milling process which they called Bellera "Air Spun." This, they claim, results in a whiter flour of more even quality.

A CROP OF TREES

The great forests of Minnesota were quickly exploited. Vast quantities of logs were taken from the forests and floated down the many streams. The exploits of the loggers were exaggerated in such tales as that of the mythical demi-god Paul Bunyan and his blue ox Babe. Legend says that Babe came to Paul in Minnesota, out of Lake Bemidji during a blue snowstorm. By 1890 Minnesota had reached first place in the country in production of lumber. The year's output for 1905 was the peak in the history of the state.

Today the state is no longer first in lumber, but the pulpwood industry is still vigorous in Minnesota, providing almost 75 percent of the total income from the state's forests. Much of this wood pulp

Minnesota's pulpwood industry provides nearly 75 percent of the total income from the state's forests. Here aspen is being loaded for pulpwood.

comes from farm woodlots. More than twenty manufacturers in Minnesota turn pulp into paper and other paper products valued at several hundred million dollars. Lumber, fuelwood, matchwood, posts, poles, veneer, railroad ties, mining timber, piling, and Christmas trees are all products of Minnesota forests. Minnesota leads all other states in the production of Christmas trees, which are grown mostly on tree farms.

Total annual value of forest products is approaching half a billion dollars.

OTHER GROWING THINGS

Farmers, working the four hundred kinds of soil found in Minnesota, produce agricultural products worth four billion dollars per year. The state leads all others in oats, sweet corn, dressed turkeys, butter, and honey for processing. It holds second place in flax and natural cheese. Flax is used mostly in the making of linseed oil; the mash is used as livestock feed.

Wheat was once the greatest of all Minnesota farm crops, and the state at one time produced more wheat than any other. Although no longer the leader, the state still produces much wheat.

Sugar beets were first grown in Minnesota in 1892 and now are an important crop. Hosts of migrant workers at one time came each year to harvest the beets, but now most harvesting is done by machine. Among other crops, the Red River Valley is noted for its potatoes, and Askov calls itself the "rutabaga capital of the world."

Livestock brings in about two-thirds of Minnesota's farm income. The livestock market at South St. Paul is ranked as the third-largest in the world. The egg and poultry exchange there is also one of the largest.

MANUFACTURING AND MINING

In 1948, for the first time, the value of manufactured products passed that of agriculture in Minnesota. Manufactured goods valued at almost seven billion dollars are produced each year in the state.

In addition to the millers, some of the other great industrial giants of the country make their headquarters in Minnesota. Minnesota Mining and Manufacturing Company pioneered in plastic adhesive tape, and now produces a wide variety of products including recording tape, copying machines and others. Minneapolis-Honeywell Company in 1885 produced the first home thermostats and is still a leader in automatic controls of all types.

The world's largest manufacturer of calendars is located in St. Paul.

The electronics industry has grown rapidly in Minnesota, and the Twin Cities today rank third in electronics among the country's metropolitan areas.

Another unusual manufacturing process pioneered in Minnesota was the method for canning whole kernel corn, patented by Big Stone Canning Company at Ortonville. Sugar beet processing is important in Minnesota. The only typha operation in the United States is carried on at Holt. The Ness Typha Company is licensed by the United States Fish and Wildlife Service to harvest cattails. The fiber is processed for insulation, upholstering, and stuffing.

Mineral production brings in over a billion dollars a year in Minnesota—dominated still by iron ore. St. Cloud is known as the "Granite City." No other region has such a large amount of colored granite. Ortonville is known for its pink granite. Frontenac stone was chosen for parts of the interior of the great Cathedral of St. John the Divine in New York City.

Sand, gravel, and cement are other important mineral products of Minnesota.

TRANSPORTATION, COMMUNICATION, TOURISM

"The squeaking could be heard for miles," said one writer in describing the Red River carts. These were platforms or wagon boxes on two large wheels, pulled by oxen. Most furs were hauled to market in these carts, and as the years went by almost every product was carried by them. Norman Kitson promoted the mass use of these carts, and at one time they went across the country in great caravans of as many as six hundred carts. Each driver was responsible for four carts, and the caravans usually had a dozen or so armed guards to protect them from Indian raids or from bandits.

The squeaking was caused by the fact that the wheels were never greased. Sometimes, when a caravan went by, the noise was so great that church services or other meetings simply had to be dismissed, since nothing could be heard and they took so long to go by. The Red River Cart era was one of the most picturesque in Minnesota history.

Another "romantic" period was that of the riverboats. By 1858 there were eleven hundred steamboats operating on the Mississippi to St. Paul. During the long winter, the ice cut off the Twin Cities from their essential boat traffic. The first boat of spring was tremendously important and a large prize was offered to the first captain to get through the massive and dangerous ice jams. In 1857 twenty boats left Galena trying for the prize. Several were crushed by shifting ice floes. The winner was a legendary figure, Captain Stephen B. Hanks, cousin of Abraham Lincoln, who won the thousand dollar prize while the city cheered.

The first steamboat on the Red River was dismantled and hauled in pieces from the Mississippi by thirty-four ox teams. Even the smaller rivers carried the passengers and commerce of the state. At one time the Rainy River had a steamboat fleet, and the Root River was a steamboat thoroughfare, with Houston a port. As time went on, many-decked excursion steamers carried happy passengers on the lakes; one of these was the *Belle of Minnetonka,* which had a capacity of thirty-five hundred in its cruises across Lake Minnetonka.

Although nearly all the paddle-wheel and stern-wheel steamers are gone, today the Mississippi River carries more freight than ever before. These days the freight is hauled in barges propelled by diesel tugs and towboats.

The first sailing craft appeared on Lake Superior in 1772. Lake traffic grew as the Sault Ste. Marie, Michigan, locks were developed. The United States government created the Duluth-Superior harbor in 1893. In 1976 it was the fourth largest port in the United States, even though it is a thousand miles from either seacoast and has a navigating season of only eight months. Almost 50,000,000 tons (nearly 45,360,000 metric tons) of freight clear the port during that time. Most of its cargoes are bulky—ore, grains, oil, or freight cars. The lake freighters have been especially designed for such bulk cargoes.

As need for overland travel grew, the stagecoach became popular in Minnesota. A blast from the coachman's horn would tell of the stage's approach, and it would soon dash into view surrounded by a cloud of dust. One of the most well-traveled stage routes ran from St. Paul to Dubuque, Iowa.

Minnesota was the birthplace of an important modern kind of "stage." Andrew G. Anderson of Hibbing bought an open car; in 1914 he found his touring car was popular for carrying passengers to the mine outside Hibbing, so he decided to charge fares. As his business grew, he became associated with Eric Wickman, who had sold him the car. Later they worked out plans for a twelve-passenger automobile coach that was built to their order. Soon they carried passengers over the fifteen-mile run to Nashwauk. By 1918 the company operated a whole fleet of buses throughout the northern part of the state. On the basis of this experience Mr. Wickman formed the company that in time grew to be the Greyhound Bus Company.

On June 22, 1862, the first engine, the *William Crooks,* pulled the first train over the first ten miles of railroad in Minnesota—from St. Paul to St. Anthony. During the early years of railroading in the state, the train crew would sometimes have to get out and tear up the fence posts along the right of way to use as fuel to keep the train going. They were generally careful to replace the borrowed fences when summer came.

Some of Minnesota's railroad tycoons were among the greatest transportation leaders of their times.

A major airline—Northwest Orient—is headquartered at the great Minneapolis-St. Paul International Airport. This airport has become one of the most important and modern in the nation.

The first newspaper published in Minnesota was the Minnesota *Pioneer,* issued on April 28, 1849. Some Ohio publishers printed the Minnesota *Register* in Cincinnati and rushed it to St. Paul, dated April 7 and April 27, both earlier than the *Pioneer,* but whether or not the dates were accurate, they were not produced in Minnesota.

Today among the many large publishing enterprises of the state is the nation's largest publisher of law books, located in St. Paul.

The fourth largest "industry" in present-day Minnesota is tourism. Today millions of travelers spend hundreds of millions of dollars every year for the privilege of enjoying the many pleasures and advantages of the state.

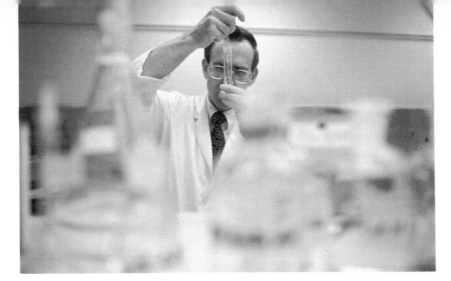

The facilities
of the Mayo Clinic
have made the city
of Rochester one
of the leading medical
centers of the world.
Above: A general
research scene in one
of the clinic's
laboratories.
Right: A surgical scene.
Below: A thematic slide
representative of
research at Mayo.

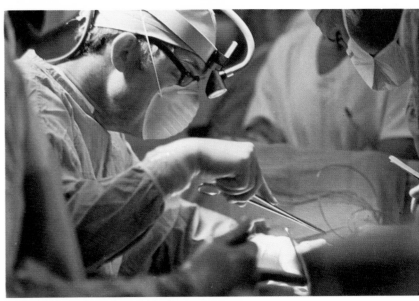

Human Treasures

ROYAL FAMILY OF ROCHESTER

Many things have made Minnesota unique but none so much as the extraordinary family genius which created a world health center in the small city of Rochester.

Dr. William Worrell Mayo, born in England, came to Le Sueur in 1855. He went to New Ulm during an Indian outbreak to help treat the wounded. To aid in his medical studies Dr. Mayo preserved the skeleton of a renegade Indian, Cut Nose.

The Mayos moved to Rochester. The Mayo sons, William J. and Charles, took an early interest in medicine and surgery and learned the bones of the body by studying the "skeleton in the family's closet." As time went on, Dr. Mayo often performed operations with the help of his young sons. Charles, at the age of nine, might be seen standing calmly on a box administering ether. The first surgical tools used by the family were made by a local blacksmith.

When he had passed fifty years of age, Dr. Mayo went to New York to brush up on the latest studies of medicine. After returning to Rochester he was so anxious to have a microscope that he mortgaged the family home for six hundred dollars to buy one; it took him ten years to repay the mortgage. However, Dr. Mayo was much in demand, and the family found means for the brothers to graduate from medical universities, after which they studied in many parts of the world.

The Catholic Sisters of St. Francis were so impressed by the family medical skill that they built a hospital in Rochester, with the senior Dr. Mayo in charge, although he then was nearing his seventieth birthday. Inspired by the fame of the Mayo family in medicine and surgery, more and more of the finest young doctors came to Rochester to study and practice. The facilities and staff, inspired by the Mayo family, grew until Rochester became one of the leading medical centers of the world. Even more important than their medical skill was the unusual ability of the Mayos to organize a vast medical "industry." They set up hospital procedures; arranged nurses' training; coordinated the work of a multitude of medical men, technicians, and other workers; organized research; and welded the whole into a smoothly running organization. More than two hundred doctors, each a specialist in his own field, now cooperate in the Mayo Clinic.

Patients now come from all over the world to the great establishments that grew from the base of the pioneering work done by the "Royal Family of Rochester." When he was eighty-seven years of age, the senior Dr. Mayo made a tour of the world. Wherever he went he was honored and received gratitude for his contributions. He died in 1911 at the age of ninety-two.

Dr. William Mayo specialized in abdominal surgery and Dr. Charles Mayo in surgery of the thyroid gland. They both died in 1939.

Other prominent Minnesota medical men include Dr. Charles A. Eastman, Dr. Justus Ohage, Dr. C. Walton Lillehie, and Dr. Charles N. Hewitt. Dr. Eastman, a Sioux, was one of the most prominent men of his race. His father was one of those who received a pardon from President Lincoln. The son was the government doctor on several Indian reservations and spent much time working with boys. He represented the Indian peoples in the 1911 London Congress of the Races. His several books include *Soul of the Indian* and *Indian Boyhood,* in which he described growing up among the Indian peoples.

Dr. Hewitt studied under Pasteur; he was one of the country's strongest promoters of public health. His most important medical contribution was the discovery of a cure for rabies, which always before had meant a certain and horrible death. Dr. Ohage was the first American surgeon to remove a gall bladder successfully, and Dr. Lillehie was a pioneer of open-heart surgery.

CREATIVE SPIRITS

One of the most notable names in literature is that of Sinclair Lewis, whose boyhood home in Sauk Centre provided the *Main*

Street title for one of his best-known works. In 1930 he became the first American ever to win the Nobel Prize for Literature.

Another noted novelist, Ole Edvart Rolvaag, taught at St. Olaf College until his death. Another writer of Scandinavian descent was Thorstein Veblen, author of works on economics and philosophy. Another novelist of great fame was F. Scott Fitzgerald. A controversial early writer was the stormy Ignatius Donnelly, who was first a politician. His novel *Caesar's Column* sold 700,000 copies, and another of his books went into 21 printings.

Minnesota gained some of its greatest fame through the work of a writer who never visited the state—Henry Wadsworth Longfellow—and his long poem *The Song of Hiawatha*. Mrs. Mary H. Eastman's work *Dacotah* was one of the sources on which *Hiawatha* was based. Another prominent woman writer from Minnesota was Margaret Culkin Banning.

Arthur Upson was gaining fame as a poet and many were predicting that he would someday rank among the greatest of American poets, when he drowned at the age of thirty-one.

Dr. F. Melius Christiansen gained world fame when he developed the a capella choir of small St. Olaf College into one of the world's finest musical organizations. Dr. Christiansen also was recognized widely for his arrangements of early church music.

The Indian peoples had a varied and interesting musical background. One of the best authorities on Indian music was Minnesota native Frances Densmore, who specialized in music of the Chippewa and Sioux.

Prominent sculptors of Minnesota have included Jacob Fjeld, Paul Manship, and James Earle Fraser. Fraser's sculpture *End of the Trail* is one of the best known ever produced in this country.

Architect Leroy S. Buffington was one of the pioneers in skyscraper construction. It was Buffington who actually received a patent in 1888 for "Iron Building Construction," providing for a building erected about girders. The most famous work of Minnesota architect Cass Gilbert is the Supreme Court building in Washington, D.C. His early fame came when he won the competition for a design of the Minnesota state capitol.

WELL KNOWN TO THE PUBLIC

James J. Hill was known as the "Empire Builder" because he developed the empire of the American Northwest and created an empire of railroads and real estate. He came to St. Paul from Canada, where he was born. His first deals were in wood fuel for the railroads; then he brought the first coal sold in Minnesota. Hill entered the transportation business by operating a steamboat on the Red River; later he purchased the bankrupt St. Paul and Pacific Railroad.

After this he pushed ahead regardless of obstacles until he realized his dream of controlling a railroad running from Minnesota to the Pacific coast and opening up the "empire" of the Northwest—the Great Northern Railroad.

Other leaders of Minnesota business and industry include milling magnate John Sargent Pillsbury; mining tycoon A.M. Chisholm; Minneapolis department store king George Nelson Dayton; and Frederick Weyerhauser, who began timbering and lumbering operations that now stretch from coast to coast and combine to make another "empire" of the Northwest.

John A. Johnson, one of Minnesota's best-loved public servants, was born in a log cabin near St. Peter. When he was elected governor, he became the first native-born chief executive of the state. He once said that the proudest moment of his life came when he earned enough money so that his mother no longer had to take in washing.

Another governor, often honored as the "Grand Old Man," was Knute Nelson, the first person born in Scandinavia ever to become a governor of a state. He was also the first Scandinavian to serve in the United States Congress and Senate. Only Knute Nelson of all Norwegian-Americans is honored by a statue in Oslo, Norway.

One of the state's most remarkable men was Henry Hastings Sibley, the first governor of the state of Minnesota. Known as "the last of the great fur dealers," Sibley was an expert on outdoor lore and especially on the Indians, who knew and greatly respected him. Once, at great hardship and personal expense, he carried supplies to a group of starving Indians through the heavy snow and ice of

Sibley House, Mendota, was the home of Henry Hastings Sibley, the first governor of the state of Minnesota.

winter. He was greatly saddened by the circumstances that required him to lead the fight against the Indians during the Sioux outbreak.

Modern Minnesota public figures include Harold Stassen, perennial candidate for high office; William O. Douglas of the United States Supreme Court; Mrs. Eugenie Anderson, the first woman ambassador in the nation's history; secretary of agriculture Orville L. Freeman; Vice-President Walter F. Mondale; and the late senator and former vice president, Hubert Horatio Humphrey.

Frank Billings Kellogg, a Minnesota senator, ambassador to Britain and secretary of state under Coolidge, won the Nobel Peace Prize for his work with French Secretary Briand in creating the Kellogg-Briand Peace Pact, a noble but unsuccessful effort to keep the world from war.

Charles Augustus Lindbergh, Jr., spent his youth in Minnesota. In the present space age, his first solo flight across the Atlantic now seems less than remarkable, but it was one of the landmarks of its age, and the excitement it caused can hardly be imagined today. His father, Charles Augustus, Sr., was a well-known Minnesota attorney, congressman, and senatorial candidate. Because he was so sincerely opposed to World War I, he lost his bid for the United States Senate. Interestingly, his son's opposition to World War II caused him to resign his army commission and temporarily lose some of the country's respect. In later years, the flier made numerous little-publicized contributions to American life.

Among the religious leaders of Minnesota were Episcopal Bishop Henry Benjamin Whipple and Catholic Archbishop John Ireland. Bishop Whipple was forty years Bishop of Minnesota and one of the greatest friends of the Indians. He was one of the pioneers for developing the idea that the Indians should be made wards of the government so that crooks and rascals would have less opportunity to cheat them.

Archbishop Ireland, born in Ireland, came to St. Paul in May, 1852. He built one of the country's notable Catholic dioceses, with his crowning achievement the great Cathedral of St. Paul.

One of the prominent Scandinavian ministers was the Reverend Eric Norelius, founder of the Lutheran church at Vasa, who started the state's first Swedish publication and came to be known as the "Father of Gustavus Adolphus College."

SUCH INTERESTING PEOPLE

The first American woman ever to become a full professor of a college was Maria L. Sanford. In her forty years on the faculty of the University of Minnesota she is credited with doing more to promote a love of literature than anyone else in the state. Another woman who gained great attention was the St. Cloud abolitionist Jane Gray Swisshelm, whose newspaper continually published violent attacks on slavery. One of the notable Minnesota women of recent days was golfer Patty Berg.

Lawrence Taliaferro, beloved Indian agent at Fort Snelling, was known to the Indians as "Four Hearts" because they said only a person with that many hearts could treat them as fairly as he did.

Notable Indians of Minnesota include chiefs White Cloud and Ukkewaus. The latter sacrified his life so that his braves could escape in the battle between Sioux and Chippewa.

Another Minnesota hero was Michael Dowling, who as a boy lost both legs, a hand, and part of the other hand in a terrible blizzard. In spite of these handicaps he became a newspaper editor, bank president, and speaker of the Minnesota House of Representatives. He performed a great service in appearing before and encouraging American and British soldiers of World War I who had lost arms or legs. The Michael Dowling School for Crippled Children at Minneapolis was created in his honor.

Among well-known Minnesota scientists was Dr. John C. Hooself, Norwegian naturalist, who carried on important work in ornithology at Lanesboro.

Theophilus L. Haecker was called the father of Minnesota dairying. He was principally responsible, also, for spreading the cooperative movement in the dairy industry. In cooperatives, by working together, farmers could set up creameries and find markets for their dairy products.

Yet another farm innovator was Oliver H. Kelley, who in 1867 founded the first national farm organization—the National Grange.

Another picturesque early figure was Joseph Renville, who lived behind a stockade at Lac qui Parle, waited on in feudal style by his army of servants. Forestville merchant Thomas Meighen gained fame for his almost legendary hospitality. He always welcomed friends from far and near, including his host of friends among the Indians.

Joseph Renshaw Brown has been called by some the "most remarkable man who ever appeared in the Northwest." Some authorities believe he is responsible for the name Minnesota. He started his career as drummer boy with Colonel Leavenworth and was one of the early explorers of the Minneapolis area. He had careers as a politician and newspaperman, and as an inventor he worked on a steam-propelled wagon long before the automobile became established. Brown's nineteen-room granite mansion was destroyed in the Sioux uprising.

General James Shields gained fame in three states as well as the nation as a whole. He served as a senator from Illinois, Missouri, and Minnesota, the only person ever elected a senator from three states.

Prominent Minnesotans in the field of entertainment include James Arness, Jane Russell, Judy Garland, Ann Sothern, Eddie Albert, Richard Carlson, and Arlene Dahl.

Teaching and Learning

The University of Minnesota, with its several branches, generally ranks among the top universities in the nation in enrollment. The achievement of Minnesota, with its relatively small population, in having a university ranking both in numbers and quality with the giant states must be considered one of the really great educational accomplishments.

The beginnings of the University of Minnesota go back to 1851, but its operations were not constant until 1869, when William Watts Folwell took over as president. From that time on its growth was steady.

One of the most notable divisions of the university is its College of Agriculture at St. Paul. Particularly outstanding is the dairy school, begun under the direction of Dr. Theophilus Haecker, one of the world's greatest dairying authorities. Helped by the leadership of the dairy school, Minnesota has become the top butter-producing state of the country. Forestry and veterinary medicine are other important activities on the agriculture campus.

In 1909 the university opened the country's first fully accredited school of nursing. In 1915, when the Mayos formed the Mayo Foundation for Medical Education and Research, this foundation affiliated with the University of Minnesota graduate school to provide the finest type of medical education and research. The university's leadership in the field of medical education was greatly enhanced by this far-sighted move.

One of the more unusual activities of the university is the operation of the St. Anthony Falls Hydraulics Laboratory, where models are designed for some of the world's largest water-control projects.

Branches of the university are located at Duluth and Morris. There are state colleges located at Winona, Mankato, St. Cloud, and Bemidji. Moorhead State University is another state institution.

For a small city to possess one college of great renown is not common. However, Northfield is probably the only city anywhere of such modest size that can boast of two colleges of international renown. Carleton College was founded at Northfield in 1866; it is now ranked in many ratings as one of the top ten liberal arts colleges of the United States. Its music department is particularly outstanding.

Also of great renown for its music is the larger St. Olaf College, opened at Northfield in 1874. Its choral music has influenced the writing and singing of vocal works throughout the world. Also well known in the musical field is Concordia College at Moorhead.

Hamline University, founded at Red Wing in 1854 under Methodist sponsorship, was the first institution of higher education in the state. After an eleven-year suspension from 1857, it was revived at St. Paul, where it still continues.

Another small city of renown in education is Faribault, which has been called the Athens of the old Northwest. Shattuck Military Academy in Faribault is outstanding in its field, as is Seabury Divinity School. St. Mary's Hall and Shattuck School at Faribault were founded by Bishop Henry Whipple.

St. John's University near St. Cloud was founded in 1857 by the Benedictine fathers and lay brothers and today is one of the largest of the order. The college library has a particularly outstanding collection of books, including many rare volumes. Nearby is St. Benedict Convent and College. Other church-related colleges include Macalester, Bethel, Augsburg, Concordia, St. Catherine's, and St. Thomas, all located in the Twin Cities; St. Teresa at Winona; and St. Scholastica at Duluth.

The teachers' education institution that opened at Winona in 1860 claims to be the first of its type founded west of the Mississippi.

Gustavus Adolphus College was begun in 1862 at Red Wing under the direction of Eric Norelius to provide "higher Christian education for Swedish-American Lutheran youth." It was moved to St. Peter where it is now located.

Formal education did not begin in Minnesota until the first school was opened at Fort Snelling in 1820 for the children of those stationed at the fort. Only twenty-nine years later the first free public schools act was passed by the territorial legislature. First territorial superintendent of schools was Edward D. Neill, called by many the father of education in Minnesota.

An interesting educational experiment in Minnesota was the Danebod Folk School opened at Tyler in 1888. This was based on the system of "folk high schools" established in Denmark by Danish theologian Grundtvig. Another experimental educational project was conducted at Owatonna by the University of Minnesota. It was an experiment in universal art education and sought to prove that all people could learn to have fuller enjoyment of many of the activities of life. The project attracted wide attention.

There are institutions for the mentally ill at St. Peter, Rochester, Fergus Falls, Anoka, Hastings, Willmar, and Moose Lake. Other state schools include those for the blind and deaf at Faribault; for dependent children at Owatonna; and for epileptics and the mentally deficient at Cambridge.

More than 86 percent of all Minnesota eighth-grade students finish high school. When compared with the national average of 65.6 percent, it is clear that many more of the people of Minnesota receive at least a high school education. In the Armed Forces Qualification Tests, Minnesota consistently led all states in scoring, indicating both the high current level of achievement and the outstanding quality of Minnesota's educational system.

Aerial view of part of the University of Minnesota campus.

Enchantment of Minnesota

MINNE-SOTAH: SKY-TINTED WATER

The very name of the state tells the visitor about many of its pleasures and attractions. Two Indian words combined, *minne* (water) and *sotah* (sky-tinted), provide the state's name. Translated, these words give Minnesota its descriptive name—Land of Sky Blue Waters. Much of the recreation of the state takes place in, on, and around these waters.

Untold thousands follow the example of Hiawatha who went "forth upon the Gitche Gumee, on the shining Big-Sea-Water, with his fishing line of cedar."

Minnesota boasts that its endless miles of canoe wilderness are the "greatest in the world," and here, also, is some of the best camping anywhere. Canoe trips are carefully planned for all—from the beginner to the expert. Autumn colors rank among the finest, and the forests become fairylands in the sparkling, feathery snow, which is perfect for skiing.

Here is the land of legend—of Hiawatha and Paul Bunyan and the other heroes of both fact and folklore. Minnesota is the goal of the famed Hiawatha Pioneer Trail, which passes through Illinois, Wisconsin, and Iowa before finally reaching the land of Hiawatha. Parts of this trail up the Mississippi Valley have been called "the second most scenic route in the United States." Carl Schurz described it in another way—"As lovely as the Rhine."

THE TWINS

One stop for almost every visitor to Minnesota is the Twin City region of Minneapolis and St. Paul. They early became popular summer resorts for wealthy and socially prominent visitors from the South and Midwest. Although there are many other twin and even triplet cities in the country, almost everyone recognizes the two Minnesota communities as *the* Twin Cities.

However, like some twins, they have almost completely different "personalities." St. Paul has been traditionally more a city of trade, commerce, transportation, and government, while Minneapolis is the industrial center. Although St. Paul is technically only seven years older, it seems to be much older and more historic than does Minneapolis.

Much of the old rivalry has died down. However, when the splendid new Metropolitan Stadium was built for the pride and joy of the Twin Cities—the Minnesota Twins baseball team—planners were careful to place it in the neutral suburb of Bloomington almost equidistant from both city centers. Also shared is the Minneapolis-St. Paul Municipal Airport.

Nor can either city claim old Fort Snelling, often called the "birthplace of Minnesota history." This now is preserved as Fort Snelling State Park, and designated as a National Historic Landmark. The famous round tower of the old fort now houses a military museum. Many of the notable events of the old Northwest took place at Fort Snelling, for thirty years the most northwesterly of all army fortifications.

In the old round tower Dred Scott was married, and he based his plea for freedom from slavery on his stay in free Minnesota. At one time Count Zeppelin, who later created the giant dirigibles that bear his name, had quarters in the old round tower at the fort. In one of his many experiments preceding the Zeppelins, the count rose from the fort parade ground in a balloon filled with illuminating gas. He soared 300 feet (91.4 meters) in a 30-minute flight.

CAPITAL CITY

Visitors to the impressive $4,500,000 capitol building of Minnesota at St. Paul may marvel at what is called the largest unsupported marble dome in the world, patterned after the great dome of St. Peter's in Rome. Few would quarrel with those who call the building one of the most beautiful of all our state capitols. St. Paul has been the home of three capitol buildings. The present capitol was

The dome of the capitol building at St. Paul was patterned after the great dome of St. Peter's in Rome. At the base of the dome can be seen the gilded sculpture showing Prosperity standing on a chariot drawn by four horses. She is holding a horn of plenty in one hand and the state symbols in the other.

completed in 1904; it is 434 feet (132.3 meters) long, and 229 feet (69.8 meters) wide. The dome is 223 feet (67.9 meters) high. At the base of the dome is a gilded sculpture known as a *quadriga.* Prosperity stands on a chariot drawn by four horses. She holds a horn of plenty in one hand and the state symbols in the other.

One of the sculptors of this group was one of America's best-known sculptors, Daniel Chester French, who also designed the six statues above the main entrance. These represent the six virtues— *Wisdom, Courage, Truth, Bounty, Integrity,* and *Prudence*—on which the work of the state is said to be based.

On the first floor, 142 feet (43.3 meters) under the ceiling of the dome, is the great Star of the North, a tremendous glass mosaic star through which the light shines when viewed either from above or below. Many well-known paintings (including those by Jean Francois Millet) and statues provide points of interest within the unique building.

The external approaches to the capitol were also the design of the building's noted architect, Cass Gilbert. At the head of the main approach are bronze statues of governors John A. Johnson and Knute Nelson.

Another notable St. Paul public building is the nineteen-story City Hall. In a great lobby extending through four stories is the mammoth Indian statue by Carl Milles representing the god of peace. This is known as the Peace Memorial Statue and weighs 60 tons (54.4 metric tons). The white Mexican onyx of the statue contrasts brilliantly with the black marble hall surrounding it. Some consider this to be the best work of the prominent sculptor. The interior of City Hall is decorated with rare woods collected from all over the world.

Another exceptional St. Paul structure is the giant Cathedral of St. Paul, one of the country's largest churches. This great edifice has been under construction since 1906 and is still incomplete.

Reminders of the city's colorful past may be found in the museum of the Minnesota Historical Society, the state's oldest organization. One of the most interesting displays is one of the historic Red River carts. Also in the museum is a picture of a St. Paul pioneer, with the inscription, "The Hon. Joe Rolette, who saved the capital for St. Paul by running away with the bill removing it to St. Peter in 1857."

St. Paul's modern Civic Arts and Science Center houses seven cultural institutions of the city—Theatre Saint Paul, School and Gallery of Art, Science Museum, Theatre Guild, Schubert Club, Civic Opera, and the Council of Arts and Sciences.

Among the parks, Como Park is outstanding; here also is the St. Paul Zoo. Indian Mounds Park preserves records of a bygone people.

The sandstone on which the city of St. Paul is built is very soft, and many caves and tunnels have been carved into it. In some of these, mushrooms are grown or cheese is cured. Many of the city's communication wires are carried through tunnels carved in the rock. St. Paul is said to be the only American city with tunnels like these.

The great Capital Centre redevelopment project in the heart of St. Paul is said to be one of the world's largest indoor shopping centers with open courts and green areas combined with an elevated pedestrian level. Buildings in the eight-block area are connected by enclosed climate-controlled pedestrian walks. One hundred and eighty acres (seventy-three hectares) on the Mississippi River have been set aside for the Riverview Industrial Park.

A complete contrast to this is St. Paul's noted "Avenue of Churches," Summit Avenue, graced by sixteen churches in a distance of only four and a half miles (a little more than seven meters).

The St. Paul Winter Carnival, begun in 1886, is found on most lists of the ten leading annual festivals of the country, ranking with such other attractions as the Mardi Gras of New Orleans. The carnival turns the city's frigid, invigorating winters into an asset. When King Winter reigns, there is a pleasing mixture of winter sports blended with the nonsensical Legends of Boreas, King of the North Wind, and Vulcan, God of Fire. There is a coronation of the Queen of the Snows as well as the traditional Grande and Torchlite parades.

Every three years the St. Paul Women's Institute conducts the Festival of Nations in which more than thirty countries take part.

More than a million visitors a year enjoy the sights, sounds, tastes, and experiences of the great Minnesota State Fair at St. Paul.

Adjacent Mendota is considered by some to be the first permanent settlement in Minnesota, the center of pioneer life of the region. At Mendota is the home of beloved Governor H.H. Sibley, the first stone house built in Minnesota, and the most famous old house in the state. The top floor was used by Sibley's friends, the Indians, as a dormitory whenever they were stopping in the vicinity.

"MINNE-HAPOLIS," CITY OF LAUGHING WATER

At one time Minnesota's largest city was known as Minnehapolis. It was given this name by Charles Hoag, who combined part of the Indian word *minnehaha,* meaning laughing water, with the Greek word for city—polis. The "h" in the name was dropped later.

In 1857, just ten years after the city was founded, a local newspaper article said, "New buildings shooting up to right and left. . . . Everyone in a hurry, such is life just now in St. Anthony and Minneapolis." The same can be said today. In proportion to its size, there is more building going on in Minneapolis than anywhere in the country except New York. The city is still hurrying forward. Nineteen of the nation's five hundred largest industries have their headquarters in Minneapolis. It ranks third in the nation in volume of its truck and rail traffic.

At first the nearby town of St. Anthony was more important than newer Minneapolis, but by 1872 the younger city had forged ahead, and the two were combined in that year.

Beyond a float in the Minneapolis Aquatennial parade can be seen one of the pedestrian walkways that link several downtown city blocks.

Throughout its history Minneapolis has had a reputation for culture. Famous people have lectured and performed there since the early days. The list includes such names as Ralph Waldo Emerson, Oscar Wilde, Mark Twain, Jenny Lind, Edwin Booth, Adelina Patti, and Ole Bull.

Today, the city is pioneering in the arts. One of the most unique and advanced theaters in the country was created for Minneapolis by the renowned theatrical expert Sir Tyrone Guthrie, for whom the theater is named. This ultra-modern looking building, in its flower-garden setting, has become a leader of the theatrical world—a place where prominent actors are proud to appear in its repertory.

Adjoining the theater is the T.B. Walker Art Center, a gift of the pioneer lumberman to the city. It houses his fine collection of Oriental art as well as his collection of paintings. The Minneapolis Institute of Arts possesses works by Rembrandt, Renoir, El Greco, Van Dyck, Rubens, Goya, and Matisse, owns Greek, Roman and Oriental treasures, and has a fine new American wing. Its white marble building is in the Greek style.

Probably the most famous cultural institution is the Minnesota Symphony Orchestra, usually ranked with the world's finest. It was founded in 1903 at the suggestion of Emil Oberhoffer, who became its first conductor. The orchestra's first president, E.L. Carpenter, was outstanding in its rapid growth. Its conductors have achieved international reputations through their work; these include Henri Verbrugghen, Eugene Ormandy, Dimitri Mitropoulos, and Antal Dorati. The orchestra's home is in Northrop Auditorium on the campus of the University of Minnesota.

Among the other interesting features of the university are the Minnesota Centennial Showboat and the Memorial Stadium, home of the university's big ten Gopher teams. The Minnesota Museum of Natural History also occupies a prominent position on the campus.

The city's public library is one of the newest and most efficient in the country.

Most attention-getting of all Minneapolis business buildings is Foshay Tower, built in the shape of the Washington Monument. This unusual building was built by utility magnate Foshay just before his public service-utility "empire" collapsed. He chose the unique form of the structure because he especially admired the Washington Monument.

The water attractions of the city have always drawn many visitors. From the beginning St. Anthony Falls was a tourist attraction. Because the limestone of the falls is so soft, the edge of the falls has moved back rapidly, and now is more than four miles (six meters) farther north than when it was first known. At one time it was near Fort Snelling. The falls might have disappeared entirely if the federal government had not built concrete reinforcements. Now the falls has lost the wild rushing natural beauty it once had and appears to be a dam.

Free concerts are given in Minneapolis parks almost nightly from Memorial Day through Labor Day.

One of the world's best-known falls is "laughing waters," Minnehaha Falls in the park of the same name. Longfellow made the falls famous by placing it near the home of his heroine, who also was named Minnehaha. When Hiawatha came to propose to Minnehaha, he "heard the Falls of Minnehaha calling to him through the silence. 'Pleasant is the sound,' he murmured. 'Pleasant is the voice that calls me.'" That pleasant voice has lured many of the world's famous to view the scenic laughing waters.

Today, in times of low water, the falls is not so "laughing" or so beautiful. When important visitors come, civic pride has been known to cause additional water to be pumped over to bring Minnehaha temporarily back to its old glory.

Minnehaha Creek drains the lake playground region at the western outskirts of Minneapolis. Best known of these lakes is Minnetonka, where once the Indians, both Sioux and Chippewa, came to worship the Great Spirit. It was one of the early fashionable resorts of the state and is still very popular. It gained great fame through one of the best-liked songs of its time. This was *By the Waters of Minnetonka* by Thurlow Lieurance. Charles Wakefield Cadman's *Land of Sky Blue Waters* also praised it in music.

Within the city itself, in the very beautiful park system alone, there are twenty-five lakes. Many of the city's residential areas also give the impression of parks, such as at Lake Harriet where some of the city's mansions gleam among their emerald lawns.

The principal annual celebration of Minneapolis is the Aquatennial, presided over by the Queen of the Lakes. Water events include championship swimming, diving, and water skiing. One of the highlights is a parade several miles long.

THE REST OF THE SOUTHERN HALF

One of the country's most unusual national monuments is Pipestone—legendary birthplace of the Indian race, the home of peace—where the peace pipe is said to have originated. The exact type of red stone of this region is found nowhere else. Today, federal

Only Indians are permitted to quarry the red stone at Pipestone National Monument. Some of them still fashion pipes from the stone. This man has just completed a pipe like the ones his ancestors carved.

law permits only the Indians to quarry the red stone at the national monument. Some of them may still be seen, painstakingly chipping out blocks to be fashioned into pipes.

Worthington is noted for its well-mounted polo team, and Fairmont is on a popular chain of eighteen lakes. Launches carry passengers through four of them. The picturesque Minnesota River Valley offers many scenic attractions as it cuts clear across the southern part of the state. In the valley, Montevideo remembers its namesake in Uruguay and puts on an interesting Spanish festival each year. Also in the valley, St. Peter is known, among other things, for being the home of five governors of Minnesota. Hutchinson has been noted for its cultural standing since its founding by the three Hutchinson brothers, a family of concert singers. Glenwood also gained artistic fame throughout the Midwest for its Bach recitals.

St. Cloud, largest city on the Mississippi north of the Twin Cities, is known particularly for its granite mines and for its industry, but its appearance is more that of a typical New England town. St. John's University and College of St. Benedict at St. Cloud are prominent educational institutions.

The city of Anoka was once the rival of the Twin Cities as the leading metropolis of the state. A stone there bears the words "Father Louis Hennepin—1680," and it is thought this may have been carved by the missionary-explorer. The Kelley Farm in Anoka

County was the home of the founder of the National Grange, Oliver H. Kelley. He carried on the affairs of the infant organization from the farm for three years.

The Canyon of the St. Croix River is known as the "Switzerland of America." The river's attractions include Interstate Park on both sides of the river, operated by both Minnesota and Wisconsin, the famous "potholes," the Devil's Chair, and the Devil's Pulpit.

Stillwater remembers the vivid days of the lumber drives down the dangerous St. Croix. In 1886 the log drive was finished just as the district court opened. The lumbermen came to town and found every bed at the Sawyer House reserved by prominent lawyers. The lumberjacks rounded them up from their beds and took them to the barroom where they were nailed to the bar by their nightshirts. Gradually the shivering lawyers were released and allowed to join an all night party.

Hastings received its greatest attention in the days of the camp meetings at nearby Red Rock, when the famous evangelists who preached there might draw as many as thirty thousand people on a single Sunday.

Red Wing takes its fascinating name from Chief Whoo-pa-doo-to, which means "Wing of the Wild Swan Dyed Scarlet." Mark Twain gave an interesting description of the Red Wing district: "There it was, this amazing region, bristling with great towns projected day before yesterday, so to speak, and built next morning. The majestic bluffs that overlook the river . . . the steep verdant slope . . . the lofty rampart of broken, turreted rocks . . . glimpses of distant villages, asleep upon capes . . . white steamers . . . and it is all as tranquil . . . as dreamland." And tranquil it has remained.

One of the principal landmarks of the entire Mississippi is the 500-foot (152.4-meter) Sugar Loaf Monolith at Winona. This attractive, shaded city is said to have had only one tree when it was established.

Winona was the scene of one of the most interesting incidents of the rough and ready steamboat days. The Mississippi cut a new channel which bypassed the landings of Winona. In a carefully laid plan the city voted to build a new stone courthouse. They loaded a barge upstream with stone, and on the way down to Winona it met with an "accident," completely blocking the new channel and bringing the trade back to Winona.

At Winona is a reminder of those days; the steamer *Julius C. Wilkie* is now permanently anchored in Levee Park.

Niagara Cave, near Harmony, largest in the Midwest, was discovered by a farmer who kept losing his pigs; one day he heard a squealing coming from a hole in the ground and found not only his pigs but the great cave as well.

Because of its vast medical facilities and relatively small size, Rochester is one of the most unusual communities anywhere. More than 200,000 people a year visit the health center. At any given time, the number of patients often more than doubles the permanent population of the city.

Owatonna was once named by the Carnegie Foundation "the typical American city." The city's National Farmers' Bank Building is widely known as one of the most interesting designs by famous architect Louis Sullivan, who was given a free hand by the bankers in spite of their doubts about what he might do to their building.

Northfield's most exciting moment in history has come to be called the "seven minutes that shook Northfield." On September 7, 1865, the Jesse James gang tried to hold up the First National Bank. When they found they could not open the safe, they became so enraged they dashed through the town firing their guns at random. Local merchants and others ran for whatever arms might be available and began firing back. Most of the gang was killed or captured, but Frank and Jesse James pulled another of their notorious escapes.

CITY OF LE SIEUR DU LHUT

The first known visitor in the region of what is now Duluth, le Sieur du Lhut, gave the city its name. As a reminder of the city's great furtrading days, the old Astor post of Fond du Lac has been recreated.

Perched on the bluffs overlooking Lake Superior, Duluth has come to be called the city in a rock garden. Its protected harbor is formed by Minnesota Point, a sandbar that stretches for six miles (nearly ten kilometers) and forms a natural breakwater. There was only one natural entrance through this sandbar, and that was six miles (nearly ten kilometers) away, between Minnesota and another sandbar on the opposite side called Wisconsin Point.

Duluth decided that it must cut an opening in Minnesota Point so that ships could enter the harbor closer to the city. The city of Superior, Wisconsin, appealed to the Army Corps of Engineers to stop this. When Duluth heard that an engineer was hurrying there with a court injunction to stop the work, it is said that all of Duluth turned out to help the steam shovel dig. The injunction arrived just after the canal had been cut through, and a little tug steamed into the harbor with its whistle shouting a triumphant note. One of the world's great aerial lift bridges now spans this opening.

The A.M. Chisholm Museum was the gift to the city of Mrs. Chisholm, widow of the iron ore pioneer. The museum developed from a children's museum that Mrs. Chisholm had established earlier. Leif Erikson Park has a statue of the Norwegian explorer and a half-size replica of his ship. Also in the park is a statue of Daniel Greysolon, known as Duluth.

One of the loveliest drives anywhere is Skyline Parkway, with its breathtaking views of the harbor below. The shoreline is spectacular in all seasons but probably never more so than when the ice breaks up in Lake Superior. Great numbers of people rush to see the huge sheets of ice tumbling, twisting, shifting, and turning, forming fantastic ice sculptures.

At Duluth the breakup of the ice means the harbor is open once again, and the arrival of the first boat is a momentous event. A Duluth church record reads: ". . . service had proceeded with due order . . . when the steamer *Keweenaw,* the first boat of the year, blew her whistle. Almost instantly the church was emptied of all but Mr. Gallagher (the pastor); whether he completed the service is not recorded; at all events, that evening after service, he made the following announcement: 'Service next Sunday morning at half past ten, Providence permitting, and if the whistle of the *Keweenaw* doesn't blow.' "

Split Rock Lighthouse, on the Lake Superior circle route in Minnesota.

From Duluth to the Canadian border, the shore of Lake Superior, on the lake circle route, is one of the scenic areas of the country. Split Rock Lighthouse on its commanding precipice presents an especially picturesque and impressive sight. In this region the metallic ores throw compasses off, making navigation difficult. At Minnesota's far northeastern tip, Grand Portage National Monument has been recreated to recall those stirring days when Grand Portage was the busiest place in the wilderness—an isolated, surprising haven of civilization.

THE REST OF THE NORTH

Northern Minnesota is a land of great contrasts—from the rocky banks of Lake Superior and the water-dotted forest wildernesses of the east to wide open spaces of the Red River Valley.

Moorhead is the metropolis of the region—the largest city in the western half of the state. One of the prize exhibits at the Clay County Historical Museum at Moorhead is a sword thought to be six hundred years old and made by the Vikings. Moorhead State University and Concordia College are important institutions of the city.

Visitors to Fergus Falls are sometimes surprised to see that its city hall is an impressive replica of Independence Hall in Philadelphia. The giant replica of the Norwegian runestone found at Kensington is a popular attraction of Alexandria. The original stone is displayed in the Runestone Museum at Alexandria.

Brainerd likes to think of itself as the home town of Paul Bunyan. At the Paul Bunyan Center in Brainerd is the largest animated statue of the giant logger ever made, and standing by is the faithful blue ox, Babe. The annual Paul Bunyan Carnival draws more than a hundred thousand visitors. Another reminder of the colorful lumbering days is Lumbertown, USA, almost thirty buildings providing a model of a lumbering community of the 1870s.

Another interesting reproduction is the Fort Mille Lacs Indian Village and Trading Post at Vineland; it features an Indian museum.

Hibbing is billed as the "Iron Ore Capital of the World." Visitors are impressed with the "Grand Canyons of the Mesabi," the tremendous open pit mines. Especially awesome is the vast canyon of the Hull-Russ-Mahoning mine, largest man-made hole in the world.

At nearby Chisholm is the Minnesota Museum of Mining. In the heart of the famed Mesabi Range, this museum features one of the finest collections of exhibits on all phases of iron mining. Beautiful Lake Vermillion near Tower is one of the principal attractions of the popular Arrowhead region. The lake with its 1,200 miles (1,931 kilometers) of woodland shore boasts 365 islands.

Ely, with its underground iron mines, is the gateway to one of America's last remaining true wilderness areas. The Superior-

Quetico primitive region, maintained on both sides of the border by the United States and Canada, has no roads in much of the area, and the only "rapid" transportation which can reach most of it is the hydroplane. Here those who love the true wilderness may find the enjoyment of woodland solitude.

Farther west the northland is still wild but many parts have touches of the outside world. International Falls has a population of 6,778. Wood pulp and paper products provide the region's greatest industry.

Another of Minnesota's great unspoiled areas is the Lake of the Woods region. Nearby Roseau is an industrial "metropolis" in spite of its small population of 2,146. Polaris Industries there makes a variety of products, the most interesting being the "snow-traveler," a motorized vehicle for winter travel in heavy snows. This was the forerunner of the snowmobile, so popular today.

West of Roseau are three Indian mounds. The Indians told a strange tale about this region. They said that at one time a group of fourteen strange people of fair complexion and light-colored hair were wrecked near this spot on the shores of a great lake which used to be there. They built sod shelters but many died during the winter, and only one man and five children managed to survive. The Indians gave them a home. The children intermarried, and the Indians said a number of their people had inherited lighter hair and skins through those unknown ancestors.

The vacation city of Bemidji is especially attractive to visitors. The huge statue of Paul Bunyan and Babe is said to be one of the country's most photographed sculptures.

Itasca State Park preserves one of the most romantic and storied areas of the North American continent. Few people are unmoved when they stand at the very spot where a small stream flows from Lake Itasca on its way to becoming the mightiest waterway in half a world—the Mississippi.

As they step from rock to rock across this tiny watercourse, they may be reminded that the river and the state which gives it birth have a common bond. From an insignificant start, both have grown quickly to an important position in the nation.

Handy Reference Section

Instant Facts

Became the 32nd state, May 11, 1858
Capital—St. Paul, settled 1840
State nickname—North Star State (formerly Gopher State)
State motto—*L'Etoile du Nord* (The Star of the North)
State bird—Common Loon *(Gavia immer)*
State fish—Walleye *(Stizostidion vitrium)*
State flower—Pink and white Lady's Slipper *(Cypripedium reginae)*
State tree—Red Pine (Norway), *Pinus resinosa*
State gem stone—Lake Superior agate
State song—"Hail! Minnesota"
Area—84,068 square miles (217,735.28 square kilometers)
Rank in nation—12th in area
Land area—80,009 square miles (207,222.51 square kilometers)
Inland waters—4,059 square miles (10,512.77 square kilometers), not including Superior
Greatest length (north to south)—405 miles (651.78 kilometers)
Greatest width (east to west)—384 miles (619.6 kilometers)
Highest point—2,301 feet (701.34 meters), Eagle Mountain, Cook County
Lowest point—602 feet (183.49 meters), Lake Superior
Number of counties—87
Population—4,286,000 (1980 estimate)
Population rank—19th
Population density—50.98 per square mile (19.68 per square kilometer), 1980 estimate
Birthrate—13.9 per 1,000
Physicians per 100,000—162
Principal cities—

City	Population
Minneapolis	434,400
St. Paul	309,714
Duluth	100,578
Bloomington	81,970
Rochester	53,766
St. Louis Park	48,922
Richfield	47,231

You Have a Date with History

1679—Sieur du Lhut (Duluth) visits region, claims it for France
1680—Father Hennepin captured
1689—First trading fort (St. Antoine) built near Lake Pepin
1727—Fort Beauharnois established, first mission begun
1731—The Verendryes explore

1763—Britain takes over
1796—Northwest Territory includes part of Minnesota
1805—Zebulon M. Pike explores, gains treaty rights
1820—Beginnings of Fort Snelling
1823—First steamboat reaches Fort Snelling
1832—Schoolcraft locates source of Mississippi
1838—First cabins at St. Paul and Minneapolis
1849—Minnesota Territory created
1851—Southern Minnesota opened for settlement
1858—Statehood
1862—Sioux war
1872—City of Minneapolis created
1884—First Minnesota iron ore is shipped
1898—Kensington runestone discovered
1905—First session of legislature in new capitol
1917—At end of World War I: 123,325 in service from Minnesota
1919—Fergus Falls tornado kills sixty
1932—Minnesota Man discovered
1946—Fort Snelling discontinued as army post
1965—Twins win American League pennant
1970—More than $1 billion has been invested in taconite plants.
1976—State's dispute with Reserve Mining nears settlement
1977—Senator Walter F. Mondale becomes vice president of the United States.
1978—Senator Hubert H. Humphrey dies

Governors of the State of Minnesota

Henry H. Sibley 1858-1860
Alexander Ramsey 1860-1863
Henry A. Swift 1863-1864
Stephen Miller 1864-1866
William R. Marshall 1866-1870
Horace Austin 1870-1874
Cushman K. Davis 1874-1876
John S. Pillsbury 1876-1882
Lucius F. Hubbard 1882-1887
A.R. McGill 1887-1889
William R. Merriam 1889-1893
Knute Nelson 1893-1895
David M. Clough 1895-1899
John Lind 1899-1901
Samuel R. Van Sant 1901-1905
John A. Johnson 1905-1909
Adolph O. Eberhart 1909-1915

Winfield S. Hammond 1915
J.A.A. Burnquist 1915-1921
J.A.O. Preus 1921-1925
Theodore Christianson 1925-1931
Floyd B. Olson 1931-1936
Hjalmar Petersen 1936-1937
Elmer A. Benson 1937-1939
Harold E. Stassen 1939-1942
Edward J. Thye 1943-1947
Luther W. Youngdahl 1947-1953
C. Elmer Anderson 1953-1955
Orville L. Freeman 1955-1961
Elmer L. Anderson 1961-1963
Karl F. Rolvaag 1963-1967
Harold E. LeVander 1967-1971
Wendell R. Anderson 1971-

Thinkers, Doers, Fighters

People of renown who have been associated with Minnesota

Anderson, Eugenia
Bierman, Bernard W. (Bernie)
Buffington, Leroy S.
Chisholm, A.M.
Christiansen, F. Melius
Dayton, George Nelson
Douglas, William O.
Fitzgerald, F. Scott
Fjeld, Jacob
Folwell, William Watts
Fraser, James Earle
Freeman, Orville L.
Garland, Judy
Haecker, Theophilus L.
Heller, Walter
Hewitt, Charles N.
Hill, James J.
Houge, Gabriel
Humphrey, Hubert Horatio
Johnson, John A.
Judd, Walter H.
Kelley, Oliver H.
Kellogg, Frank Billings

Lewis, Sinclair
Lillehie, C. Walton
Lindbergh, Charles Augustus
Manship, Paul
Mayo, Charles Horace
Mayo, Charles W.
Mayo, William J.
Mayo, William Worrell
Mondale, Walter F.
Nelson, Knute
Ohage, Justus
Pillsbury, John Sargent
Rolvaag, Ole Edvart
Sanford, Maria L.
Shields, James
Sibley, Henry Hastings
Stassen, Harold
Upson, Arthur
Veblen, Thorstein
Weyerhauser, Frederick
Wickman, Eric
Youngdahl, Luther

Annual Events

January—Winter Carnival, Winona
January-February—Winter Carnival, St. Paul
June—Peony Show, Faribault
June—Fiesta Days, Montevideo
July—Aquatennial, Minneapolis
July—Steamboat Days, Winona
July-August—Song of Hiawatha Pageant, Pipestone
July-August—Passion Play of the Pines, Chisholm
August—Timbertennial, International Falls
August-September—State Fair, St. Paul

90

Index

94

PICTURE CREDITS

Color photographs courtesy of the following: James Jerome Hill Reference Library, 8; Minnesota Department of Economic Development, 11, 12, 19, 27, 29, 39, 42, 48, 49, 52, 57, 67; Duluth Convention and Visitors Bureau, 51, 85; Mayo Clinic, 62; St. Paul Area Chamber of Commerce, 75; Minneapolis Chamber of Commerce, 78; Minneapolis Park and Recreation Board, 79; Architect of the U.S. Capitol, 22; Pipestone National Monument, 81.

Illustrations on back cover by Len W. Meents.

ABOUT THE AUTHOR

With the publication of his first book for school use when he was twenty, **Allan Carpenter** began a career as an author that has spanned more than 135 books. After teaching in the public schools of Des Moines, Mr. Carpenter began his career as an educational publisher at the age of twenty-one when he founded the magazine *Teachers Digest.* In the field of educational periodicals, he was responsible for many innovations. During his many years in publishing, he has perfected a highly organized approach to handling large volumes of factual material: after extensive traveling and having collected all possible materials, he systematically reviews and organizes everything. From his apartment high in Chicago's John Hancock Building, Allan recalls, "My collection and assimilation of materials on the states and countries began before the publication of my first book." Allan is the founder of Carpenter Publishing House and of Infordata International, Inc., publishers of *Issues in Education* and *Index to U. S. Government Periodicals.* When he is not writing or traveling, his principal avocation is music. He has been the principal bassist of many symphonies, and he managed the country's leading non-professional symphony for twenty-five years.